WHAT WORKS WHEN

Life

DOESN'T

Stuart Briscoe

This book is designed for your personal reading pleasure and profit. It is also designed for group study. A leader's guide with helps and hints for teachers and visual aids (Victor Multiuse Transparency Masters) is available from your local bookstore or from the publisher.

VICTOR

BOOKS a division of SP Publications, Inc.

WHEATON. ILLINOIS 60187

Offices also in
Whitby. Ontario. Canada
Amersham-on-the-Hill. Bucks. England

Twelfth printing, 1983

Scripture quotations are from the King James Version of the Bible.

Library of Congress Catalog Card Number: 75–26443
ISBN: 0-88207-725-2

VICTOR BOOKS
A division of SP Publications, Inc.
Wheaton, Ill. 60187

Contents

To Mary, my mother,
who brought me to life,
who led me to Christ,
who taught me to work,
who inspired me to preach,
and who,
during the preparation of this manuscript, has
battled cancer with
quiet courage and unshaken faith
proving once again she knows
"what works when life doesn't"

Foreword

Stuart Briscoe has the rare gift of explaining the unchanging truths of Scripture in fresh and insightful ways. These expository messages skillfully relate some well-known Psalms to the teachings of other parts of the Bible. The result is a statement faithful to the whole counsel of God and characterized by pertinent illustrations drawn from a life enriched by meaningful experiences with the Lord and with His people.

Both in style and in content the chapters of this book reflect the pulpit and pastoral ministry that has made Stuart Briscoe's service for the Lord unusually fruitful. Because of this, what he has to say should be applicable to a wide spectrum of interests and needs.

A number of these messages were given by Stuart Briscoe in the week of special services held at Wheaton College in April, 1975. The response of students, faculty, and staff alike was an eloquent testimonial to the pertinence of such ministry for our times.

The contents of this book declare the Word of God. Thus what has been written deserves thoughtful and prayerful attention. This will ensure that the expectations of the author and the publisher will be fulfilled in the edification of the reader for personal blessing and for the glory of God.

Hudson T. Armerding, Ph.D.
President, Wheaton College

Preface

You may be about to experience one of the biggest surprises of your life. No, don't look around, just keep reading!

It has to do with the Psalms. For many years I regarded them almost as optional extras to mainline spiritual truth. The sort of thing you read when you are too sick to concentrate or too tired to keep awake for more than a few minutes. I enjoyed singing them with Presbyterians, chanting them with Episcopalians, quoting them to the dying, and reading them in my devotions. But they were little more than the frosting on the cake—the work of mystical poets mixed in with the "important" work of realistic theologians to make it a little more palatable.

Oliver Cromwell asked the Scots to "think it possible you may be mistaken." To which I, though not a Scot, would have to reply, "Oliver, if you're listening, when it comes to the Psalms I was mistaken." My problem was that though I had read, sung, chanted, and warbled the Psalms, I had never *studied* them. When I did, I had my big surprise!

I became so excited with my study of the Psalms that I embarked on a series of sermons to the congregation of Elmbrook Church, a series which lasted almost a year. So many people expressed the same surprise that I had felt. "I never realized how clearly the Psalms speak to the issues of our day," they said.

Considerably emboldened by this response, I took the Psalms with me on tours to mission fields in the Orient and South America. Missionaries expressed the same surprise. "We always read the Psalms before going to sleep at night but never studied them as God's word to us for day-by-day activities."

The same thing happened among students on such campuses as Wheaton College and Columbia Bible College. "We didn't realize the clarity of the world view expressed in this part of the Bible," was the sort of statement I heard regularly from them.

I enjoy giving after-dinner speeches to businessmen, speaking in school assemblies (where permitted), in fact, talking anywhere to anybody who will listen. And do you know what I discovered? People in all sorts of situations are interested to know what God has to say through the Psalms.

"Telling the Truth" is our weekly radio broadcast, released in many parts of the world. You'll never guess the series that has elicited the biggest response! "In Reality" was our weekly TV show. Would you like to hazard a guess as to the area of Scripture I have used more than any other as I have talked on subjects such as death, depression, and fear? You're right. The Psalms.

When the editor of Victor Books invited me to submit a manuscript, I talked to him about the Psalms. He wasn't too sure about the idea, because traditionally the Psalms have not been the most popular Scriptures for study. But he and his colleagues decided to go ahead and "give it a whirl." So here we are with some studies that really show how the Bible presents "what works when life doesn't."

My thanks to all who have participated with me in the development of these studies—from the venerable C. H. Spurgeon, to students at Wheaton and missionaries in Venezuela, the congregation at Elmbrook, unknown thousands on radio and TV, and Georgia Douglass, who translated my "typing" into typing and my English English into the American variety.

Psalm 1

Blessed is the man that walketh not in the counsel of the ungodly, nor standeth in the way of sinners, nor sitteth in the seat of the scornful. But his delight is in the law of the Lord; and in His law doth he meditate day and night.

And he shall be like a tree planted by the rivers of water, that bringeth forth his fruit in his season; his leaf also shall not wither; and whatsoever he doeth shall prosper.

The ungodly are not so, but are like the chaff which the wind driveth away. Therefore the ungodly shall not stand in the judgment, nor sinners in the congregation of the righteous.

For the Lord knoweth the way of the righteous, but the way of the ungodly shall perish.

1

When Happiness Eludes You

When an old lady in the Deep South asked me whether we have a Fourth of July in England, my immediate response was, "No, Madam, we go straight from the third to the fifth!"

I learned my history in England, and when I came to this country, I knew so little about the events of 1776 that I wouldn't have recognized a Declaration of Independence if I'd tripped over it. But times have changed. Now I know that the Declaration of Independence says man has three unalienable rights: "life, liberty, and the pursuit of happiness." But I have often wondered why there are so many unhappy people in a country where freedom to pursue happiness is one of the most cherished rights.

What Is Happiness Anyway?

One reason so many people are unhappy is that, though they are busy pursuing happiness, *they aren't sure what it is*. People want to be happy but most of those I talk with seem to think that happiness will come their way when everything else starts to go their way. It's the happiness that says, "I've got a wonderful feeling, everything's going my way . . . ," but life isn't like that except in "Oklahoma." There is no way that anyone can expect everything always to go his way. So if happiness is related to that kind of situation, we must settle for a fair measure of unhappiness.

The Bible shows, however, that happiness is not necessarily related to happenings, and that it ıs possible for people to be happy in difficult and unpleasant circumstances. Paul talked a lot about joy when he was in prison. The Lord Jesus told His disciples to "rejoice and be exceeding glad" when they were persecuted because they belonged to Him. So it is obvious that happiness and joy are more than good feelings that result from pleasant circumstances.

The Greeks were of the opinion that their gods were having a great time. They used the word *makarios* (blessed) to describe it. It means to be "enriched, contented, and fulfilled."

This word appears in the New Testament in such verses as "Blessed are the poor in spirit" (Matt. 5:3). The Greek translation of Psalm 1 uses the same word: *"Blessed* is the man who walks not in the counsel of the ungodly, nor stands in the way of sinners, nor sits in the seat of the scornful" (v. 1).

Where Is Happiness Found?

The psalmist here makes it quite clear that man will *not* find happiness in certain areas. That gives us another clue why many people aren't finding happiness. They don't know *where to seek it.* People who are free to pursue happiness will not find it if they don't know what it is, or if they chase it where it isn't.

It was January 1 when I arrived on my first visit to the United States. I turned on the television and saw a picture the like of which I had never seen before. It was a rear view shot of a row of big men in tight pants bending over in such a fashion that they appeared to be putting intolerable strain on said pants.

Behind them stood a man who seemed to have lost his temper completely. He was yelling and shouting, apparently because the other men had his ball and he wanted it back. Eventually, after much shouting, they gave it to him. He promptly gave it to one of his friends who ran a few steps and was treated to an awful beating by some other men wearing similar tight pants, but of a different color.

They were apparently very sorry about their behavior because, after they had beaten him up, they gathered in a small group to pray about it. They were not sincere, however, because they went straight back and did the same thing again.

After repeating this whole outrageous procedure about 10 times, the man with the ball suddenly threw it about 60 yards to another man I hadn't noticed before. He caught it, ran a few yards, did a funny little dance, and the crowd went wild. I thought I had stumbled on some religious festival (subsequently I discovered I was right!) and was completely mystified until someone started to explain what was happening so that a newly arrived Englishman could understand.

It appeared that the quarterback had so effectively faked a hand-off to his running back that the defensive line and linebackers had played the run, leaving the receiver wide open to catch the pass and go in for a touchdown. And it all happened because the defensive players chased the man without the ball.

The moral of the story is, if you are free to pursue happiness, don't be faked into pursuing it where it isn't!

"The Counsel of the Ungodly"

"Blessed is the man who walks not in the counsel of the ungodly," means happiness isn't found in a life-style that leaves out God. An atheist has a godless philosophy. He chooses to believe that God does not exist. He does this by faith, quite obviously, because he has no concrete evidence that there is no God. But the atheist has a major problem. If there is no God behind the universe, there is no reason behind his own existence. Both he and his world are products of fate, the chance products of meaningless events.

"Are you alive?" was the question I posed to a teenager in a coffee-house one evening.

"Yes," he said, looking startled.

"Why are you alive?" was my next question.

"Because I was born and haven't died."

"Did you have anything to do with your birth?"

"No, except I was there!"

"Do you plan on having anything to do with your death?"

"No."

"Then as far as you are concerned, your birth was an accident and your death will be an accident."

"I suppose you're right."

"Then I know what you are. You are an accident suspended between accidents."

He looked thoughtful for a moment and said, "You know something, that helps me understand myself better than anything I've heard."

Many people do not believe there is a God behind their birth, who plans for them in life and who wants one day to take them to be with Him. They are therefore faced with the unpleasant prospect of having no real point to their existence. They must either sink into despair as a result, or do anything that will help them to stop thinking seriously.

A godless philosophy produces some people who give up on life and others who try to keep themselves going by filling their nagging emptiness with trivialities. Either way, the people concerned are not fulfilled. It's difficult to believe you are a meaningless accident and to feel good about it!

"The counsel of the ungodly" does not refer only to the philosophies of atheists, however. It can also describe the way of life adopted by church people who give lip service to God but don't feel it necessary to regard God as God. The whole concept of God assumes that He is supreme, that He's the greatest. But it is too easy to "believe" in the "Supreme One, the Greatest" and refuse to give Him supreme place in one's life. This is an approach to life that is little more than atheism with an ecclesiastical façade.

So you can be an atheist, Baptist, Methodist, Adventist, or any other "ist" and still live according to the "counsel of the ungodly." This breeds a serious conflict between the knowledge of God's requirements and the refusal to obey. Tension results and severe unhappiness and discontent inevitably follow. There's no happiness in a godless philosophy, however you look at it.

"The Way of Sinners"

Happiness is not to be found "in the counsel of the ungodly" as we have seen. Neither is it to be found "in the way of sinners." Most people seem to think that a sinner is someone who does what they don't do! This position is comfortable but false. Like a first-class seat on the wrong plane.

From the biblical perspective, a sinner is a person who "misses the target" so far as achievement is concerned or "misses the point" so far as truth is concerned. So a sinner has severe problems.

God has given men a target and men keep missing it. Many of them know they are failing and in all sincerity keep trying and missing. This is terribly frustrating for them. They feel guilty and helpless and decidedly unhappy.

But some are not aware of God's standards, so they are not aware that they are missing them. They don't even know what they're supposed to be hitting. This reminds me of an experience in my marine training. We were taken to the firing range in the middle of the night and told to engage in "night firing." The main problem we encountered was that we couldn't see any targets. What an exercise in futility!

The person who does not have God at the base of his thinking will have no guidelines at the root of his behaving. And that is as unfulfilling as it is frustrating.

"The Seat of the Scornful"

If you walk long enough and then stand around for a while you will soon need a comfortable seat. Look where the person who walks in the counsel of the ungodly and stands in the way of sinners finds himself: "in the seat of the scornful."

This comes as no surprise. Godless philosophy leads to a sense of purposelessness and a life-style that is frustrating, but there is a limit to the purposelessness and frustration that most people can take. Sooner or later they give up and become hard-boiled cynics. They scoff at any suggestion that God is real; they scorn any standards that purport to come from God; and they minimize the efforts of God's people to bring a message of hope to the hopeless and comfort to the troubled.

We live in a cynical age. People are cynical of most institutions, many politicians, and much theology. They laugh at moral standards and attack divine principles. But they put little of value in the vacuum they create, and their cynicism not only leads to increased societal anguish but it rarely brings much joy to the cynics themselves.

"The Law of the Lord"

"But" is a great little word! It's a key word in Bible study for it alerts the reader to the fact that there is another side to what has just been said, and it is about to be presented.

So far the psalmist has been at great pains to state where happiness isn't. Now he speaks positively about the direction in which happiness can be sought and found. "But his delight is in the law of the Lord" (v. 2) gives the clue that so many people need to discover.

According to the slogan, "Happiness is . . ." a rubber duck, a benign tumor, and other assorted things and experiences. But the happiness we are talking about is "relationship to the Lord." Just as godless philosophy is doomed to disappointment, the opposite view leads to the opposite experience. Instead of taking a plea of faith and deciding that God isn't, man must take the leap of faith and believe He is.

It is worth noting that the Bible makes no attempt to prove that God is. It simply starts by saying "In the beginning God . . . " and then develops that theme for 66 whole books. The evidence for reasonable faith that God does exist is piled high for all but the totally obdurate to believe.

But having said that happiness is to be found in the area of belief that "God is," we must add that the God of whom we speak is not a vague force or a creative influence but One who speaks to man through His law.

The law of the Lord refers to God's requirements for man. What man should do, what he should not do. It stipulates what will happen if he does and what he can expect if he doesn't.

Imagine what it would be like if you had to earn your living by playing football but the game in which you played had no ball, no goals, no sidelines, no hash marks, no rules, no scores, no officials, no spectators, no end, and no result. You would have to play day after day of meaningless nonsense, dragging yourself out of bed morning by morning, steeling yourself for another day of unmitigated nothingness.

Now think of the difference that rules and goals and officials and results make. The godless philosophy wants you to play the first "game," but the "law of the Lord" ensures the second kind of game. And there is no comparison.

Of course, you have to know the rules, and that is why the fulfilled person not only knows the Lord has spoken but he "delights" in what He has said and assiduously learns and follows the instructions.

It's one thing to "meditate day and night" but it's another to play according to the rules. This is where we tend to come unglued. No person alive has fully followed through on all God's requirements.

The measure in which we fail to fulfill the law is the measure of our sin and responsibility. But even here there is more opportunity to be joyful, for those who acknowledge their sin and seek the Lord can experience forgiveness, because Christ died that we might be forgiven. There is no more happy person than the one who knows what he should be and knows he hasn't been it but has confessed and been forgiven. "Blessed are they whose iniquities are forgiven, and whose sins are covered. Blessed is the man to whom the Lord will not impute sin" (Rom. 4:7-8).

After the Lord has done His great forgiving work, He sends the Holy Spirit to live in the forgiven sinner. The Holy Spirit is the One who inspired the law of the Lord in the first place, and when He comes into a person's life, He begins to impart the power to obey the law of the Lord. Paul said, "The righteousness of the law [is] fulfilled in us, who walk not after the flesh, but after the Spirit" (Rom. 8:4).

There is something very attractive and distinctive about such a life. Particularly when it is contrasted with so many of the hard, harsh, cynical, unhappy lives produced by those who sit in the seat of the scornful.

"Like a Tree"

The psalm moves into a description of the fulfilled life with the words, "And he shall be like a tree planted by the rivers of water" (Psalm 1:3). I've always loved trees, possibly because my early boyhood was spent in the English Lake District. By the lakes and rivers the trees are tall and straight, but up in the mountains many of them appear to be hanging on the sides of precipices, solely concerned with survival. The difference, of course, is in the hidden source of their water supply.

People are like that for the same reason. Without their roots deep into the river of God they are fully occupied endeavoring to cope with the chill winds and raging storms of their unfortunate circumstances. But the same storms and winds fail to ruffle the composure or threaten the stability of the person planted by the river.

There are some people whose lives under strain are so unusual that others are amazed at the strength they exhibit and the sense of deep joy they exude. And it is all attributable to the work of the Spirit of God.

Fruit in Season

Trees and people are expected to do more than stand around looking tall and straight. They are supposed to produce. In fact, there is no way that a totally unproductive person can be fulfilled or happy. Many have tried to be happy and lazy, but they have failed, because God made human beings to be productive.

Recently, I appeared on a TV show dealing with the subject of work. A young girl wrote in and said:

I work in a gas station and I don't always feel like getting up at 5 A.M. 'cause it's still dark outside and stuff, but once I get some cereal in my stomach and get going I'm OK. I may not have the most beautiful job in the world but I'm doing a service for other people for the glory of God. If I would go to work with a crummy attitude and be mean and crabby to all my customers, they would go to their jobs and families and be crabby too. Just think of all the people this would affect. There would be one bad chain reaction, but I pray that each day I will give good service and a friendly smile to all my customers.

How would you like to work at a filling station at 6 in the morning in a Wisconsin winter? Do you think you could be happy?

You could if you were convinced that God had put you there like a tree by the river.

You would also be able to "bring forth fruit in season." Fruit is the external evidence of internal life. Oranges growing on branches lead one to assume that the branches belong to an orange tree. People rooted in the Spirit of God work in the power of the Spirit, and the fruit shows in their work and their attitudes. "Love, joy, peace . . . " begin to sprout all over the place. It's the happy life.

Leaves That Don't Wither

Trees look great in the fall so long as you don't look too closely. But if you do happen to get close you will find that the glorious colors are the colors of death. The once-fresh green leaves are heading for the ground to drive people into a frenzy of raking and burning. It's a pity it has to be like that because some trees don't behave that way. They are evergreens. They don't start with fragrant freshness in the spring, curl up in the heat of summer and fall in fall, before retiring into their bark for the winter. They keep going. "Their leaf shall not wither." They exhibit consistency and quiet determination.

Our Lord Jesus was a beautiful example of not withering. When Peter "advised" Him not to go to Jerusalem, He made it abundantly clear that He was going. When He got to Jerusalem He quietly and methodically put His affairs in order. He gave final instructions to His disciples, prayed about their situation, talked with the Father, and kept going relentlessly toward His goal. Pilate couldn't move Him. Herod couldn't get anywhere with Him. The mob in the garden seemed to come under His authority.

Even on the cross He didn't wither. He refused the anesthetic offered to Him, dealt with the needs of His mother, and prayed for His enemies. When He was through, He still didn't wither. With a great shout, He dismissed His spirit.

Now we can't go that far, but we can live a whole lot nearer to it than we do. The same Holy Spirit through whom Christ offered Himself to God is the river of our resource to make us like evergreen trees.

Prosperity

"And whatsoever he doeth shall prosper," must surely be one of the most titillating promises in Scripture. This is because we tend to equate prosperity with wealth and wealth with money. Many people take this promise as a divine guarantee that if they do things God's way they will make their fortune. In fact, it is not uncommon to hear some businessmen attribute their wealth to their godliness. This kind of thinking must be treated with care, because the Bible points out that the "love of money is the root of all evil" (1 Tim. 6:10). More money for some people would mean more temptation than they could handle, which would lead to disaster, not prosperity.

It is far more beautiful to see that God is promising prosperity of life rather than of bank accounts. He is assuring those who obey Him and honor Him that in their obedience and trust they will find enrichment of life. This will mean far more to their true happiness than any amount of material prosperity.

Joseph was sold as a slave, but as a slave he honored God and God prospered him. The Lord didn't set him free at once and he didn't make a personal fortune but he changed the course of a nation and altered human history. Through Joseph's servitude in Egypt, God was able to get the children of Israel into Egypt, so that He could later get them out and into the Promised Land.

Recently, I counseled a couple who have gone through deep water since they committed their lives to Christ. They have been sincere in their commitment and careful in their discipleship, but it hasn't led to material prosperity. Illness has not been banished from their experience. Persecution in terms of loss of job has come their way. Nevertheless, they have prospered. As people, they are deeper, more contented, and better able to cope with life. They believe God is prospering them in the way that He wants them to go.

A Word of Warning

The psalmist sounds a somber note as well as a happy one. "The ungodly are not so" (v. 4). There is a chill about those words *not so*. All the majestic themes that have been applied to the life of the believer are shown to be irrelevant to the unbeliever. He can hear all that has been said and then understand that none of it applies to him. He must understand that his life will be as empty as the "chaff which the wind drives away." He will "not stand in the judgment" (which does not mean he will not be there, but that he will be there and he won't have a leg to stand on) and he will not be "in the congregation of the righteous."

In short, "the way of the ungodly shall perish." This means that the believer's joy is always tinged with pain. While he enjoys the riches of forgiveness and the resources of the Spirit, he is surrounded by those who are impoverished in soul and defeated in spirit. While he lives a fruitful, consistent life, he meets with those who are disenchanted and discouraged.

The Christian does not ignore or dismiss the ungodly but for Christ's sake loves them and endeavors to share with them the alternatives that God offers. Dives "fared sumptuously" while Lazarus was dying miserably (see Luke 16:19-31). Not so the happy man. He shares his joy and reaches out to those who are perishing.

The Lord Knows

Above and beyond everything else, the believer has the calm settled assurance that all is well and that God is honoring the one who honors Him. This assurance is more conducive to real happiness than we can imagine. But to realize that "God knows the way of the righteous" which leads to heaven ("the congregation of the righteous"), is even more thrilling. It means that the Lord is in control of every situation into which His obedient child moves, and that every step of the way is leading inexorably to glory.

Psalm 2

Why do the heathen rage, and the people imagine a vain thing? The kings of the earth set themselves, and the rulers take counsel together, against the LORD* and against His anointed, saying, "Let us break their bands asunder, and cast away their cords from us."

He that sitteth in the heavens shall laugh: the Lord shall have them in derision. Then shall He speak unto them in His wrath and vex them in His sore displeasure. "Yet have I set My King upon My holy hill of Zion."

I will declare the decree: the LORD hath said unto Me, "Thou art My Son; this day have I begotten Thee. Ask of Me, and I shall give Thee the heathen for Thine inheritance, and the uttermost parts of the earth for Thy possession. Thou shalt break them with a rod of iron; Thou shalt dash them in pieces like a potter's vessel."

Be wise now, therefore, O ye kings: be instructed, ye judges of the earth. Serve the LORD with fear, and rejoice with trembling. Kiss the Son, lest He be angry, and ye perish from the way, when His wrath is kindled but a little.

Blessed are all they that put their trust in Him.

---

* In Psalms 2 and 8, LORD when referring to Jehovah is set in all capitals to aid in pointing out the distinction between Lord and LORD made by the author. Elsewhere in the book the publisher's usual style, Lord, is followed.

2

When the World Is Falling Apart

There was a time when believers who asked questions were treated with suspicion. The inference was that they wouldn't need to ask questions if they really believed. However, it is now permissible to have an inquiring mind, so, hopefully, more people with a more intelligent faith may have greater impact on our world.

However, many believers still do not ask enough questions. It may be they just aren't interested enough to think through their faith. Or, perhaps, they are so insecure in the Lord that any difficulty puts intolerable strain on their experience.

Whatever the case might be, there is no doubt that the psalmist was very free in his questioning about many things going on in his world that made him think. He asked two big questions that need to be asked and answered today, as in every generation. The first question was . . .

"Why Do the Heathen Rage?"

If that conjures up mental pictures of naked savages dancing around the pot waiting for the missionary to be thoroughly stewed, you don't quite have the right idea!

The Jews knew that God had chosen them to be key people in His plan for the human race, but they had allowed things to go to their heads a little. They felt that they were *the* people and all the rest were "heathen." Accordingly, when they talked about "heathen," they were not thinking about savages but the nations of the world.

The word *rage* has the connotation of a "raging sea," so the question is really, "Why is there so much international conflict?" I believe that every thinking person in our world ought to be asking this question. Not least, the believers. Unrest and bloodshed are on every hand. The horror of war has become so commonplace now that we can sit at home eating supper while watching the latest carnage graphically portrayed on our television screens.

How many people are asking deep questions as to the cause of all this senseless belligerence? Why does the Middle East have to be constantly seething? Was there any reason for the hopeless prolongation of the Indochina conflict? Can peace ever come to the Emerald Isle? Will the tribal antagonisms of the African continent continue to ferment and possibly erupt in a dread holocaust? What is going to happen? Will it ever end? Is there any hope? Why is there so much conflict?

"Why Do the People Imagine a Vain Thing?"
The second question is as momentous as the first. "Why do the people imagine a vain thing?" Remember that when the Bible talks about "vanity" it is not referring to the amount of time spent in front of a mirror trying to make up for the ravages of time. *Vanity* in the Old Testament means "emptiness, futility, confusion." The question really is, "Why is there so much individual confusion?"

• Why do so many people carefully study their horoscopes when it is pretty obvious that horoscopes are 90% nonsense and 10% worse than nonsense.

• Why are so many young people, and not so young people, getting off into Eastern mysticism? Maharaj Ji can do his thing in the Astrodome and attract thousands of devotees.

• How can Sun Myung Moon talk hundreds of young people into marriages with people whom they have barely met, by promising some kind of spiritual bonus?

• Why do we see baldheaded kids in saffron robes peddling their books at the major airports and on street corners, offering "the highest knowledge" to the gullible?

Desperate couples trapped in marriages that have degenerated into deadlock in the name of wedlock are trying all kinds of cures.

- Sexual surrogates sell their addlebrained therapy.
- Open marriage is touted as the way to "meaningful relationships," but simply opens a Pandora's box of social and sexual ills.
- "Creative divorce" is seriously propagated as an answer to marital unhappiness.

Spiritual, social, and philosophical confusion abounds and shows no sign of abating.

There is a real danger that believers might adopt an attitude of calculated indifference to these problems. Christians may feel that they are all right personally, and doubt whether they can change anything anyway. This indifference would be understandable if there were no answers, but since there are answers available, it is totally inexcusable.

Kings and Rulers

In true rhetorical fashion the psalmist answers his own questions before anyone can get a word in! "The kings of the earth set themselves, and the rulers take counsel together." When this psalm was written, kings and rulers were able to exert great influence on the people and lead them for good or ill in the direction they chose. Today we have leaders and charismatic personalities who are able to move far more people than the old-time kings and rulers.

The mass media has produced a whole new situation in our contemporary society. Talk show hosts can sell their philosophies of life to millions without moving from their ornate sets. The celebrity guests of talk shows, who start in the seat of honor and slowly slide to oblivion off the end of the couch, are able to influence thousands of marriages by sharing their experiences. Often their chief "qualification" for such monumental exposure may be an ability to outstrip a defensive secondary or to win a political primary.

The kings and rulers of our day do not sit on thrones or lead their men into battle. Many of them sit in Madison Avenue offices dispensing their philosophy of life in million-dollar advertising campaigns. They work feverishly in smoke-filled studios in Nashville, turning out LPs that will shape the thinking of millions. Or from their luxurious penthouses they plan the articles that will hit the newsstands in slick, sophisticated formats.

Whoever today's kings are and wherever they meet, most of them have one thing in common: "They take counsel together." That is, their whole approach to life and, accordingly, the influence they exert on the masses, is contrary to the Lord's ways. They consult themselves, not God. What they have to offer is the product of their thinking. Accordingly, the masses hear more of the voice of fallible man than of the infallible God. They are imbibing more error than truth. They learn to adore men, not God, and serve mammon rather than the Lord.

There is, of course, the possibility that men and women of real spiritual caliber may take places of influence and lead people in the paths of righteousness. But it is more possibility than probability. It just isn't happening to any marked degree, and we had better recognize it!

"Against the LORD"

The psalmist had no doubt that the leaders of his day were "against the LORD and against His anointed." Their hostility to the LORD was open. They saw no reason to hide it, and they didn't try. It is important that we should understand this hostility, because the situation is the same today as it was then.

When LORD appears in capital letters in the King James Version, it signifies the name of Israel's God, Jehovah or Yahweh. The great name Jehovah, regarded by the Jews as too sacred to fall from their lips or even to flow from their pens, is obscure in its origin, but we do know that it has to do with God's eternal, unique being. "I am that I am" (Ex. 3:13-14). Probably, "I will be what I will be" is more accurate.

Either way, the name of Jehovah conveys a great sense of independence, self-sufficiency, and determination. It suggests, "I am what I am, I'll do what I'll do, and I'll accomplish what I please!" It gives warning to man that he had better not confuse God with anyone else or try to take God's place.

It should be obvious that the very idea of a self-existent, self-dependent, totally unique God does not appeal to men who see themselves in those capacities. Self-sufficient man doesn't want to hear about self-existent Jehovah. Self-determined man has nothing but hatred for a message that is based on the statement that God is the One who determines. So arrogant leadership will always be opposed to any statement concerning Jehovah.

"And Against His Anointed"

The title *Christ,* given to the Lord Jesus, is closely related to the Greek word *Christos,* which means "Anointed One." In fact, Psalm 2:1-2 was quoted by the early disciples in the prayer recorded in Acts 4:25-26 and the *Anointed* of the psalm becomes the Lord Jesus in that prayer. It is not surprising, then, that in our world there is not only hostility to the very idea of Jehovah but also great resistance to the biblical message of Christ.

In Old Testament times, men were anointed as prophets, priests, or kings to show that they had God's approval and were acting as God's agents. Jesus Christ came as God's agent par excellence. His ministry was to reign over more people than any king, reveal more truth than any prophet, and lead more sinners to reconciliation than any priest. In short, He came to do for man what man cannot do for himself. He came to redeem. Self-sufficient men, wrapped up in their own schemes, content with their sins, and bent on living their own lives, don't want to know about a Redeemer. The last thing they want to hear is that a Saviour has come. They look for answers down here, so they have no time for a Christ who came as the answer from up there.

Painful as it is for the believer to realize, he lives in a world which is basically opposed to God's revelation that He is Jehovah and His Son is Lord. For contemporary society to admit these two things would mean a complete reversal of its thinking and a total revolution in life-style.

Cords and Bands

The leaders of mankind are vocal. The opinion makers are busy making opinions and selling them attractively packaged. And listen to what they are saying: "Let us break their bands asunder, and cast away their cords from us" (v. 3). The cords and bands that they wish to get rid of are the principles and standards of Jehovah and His Christ.

It is interesting to note that much of contemporary philosophy is as old as David's era. In fact, it's older. It's as old as Adam. He decided to get rid of the cords and bands, anticipating that he would be enriched as a result. But he got the idea from Lucifer. Lucifer was once a beautiful angel who had a superb position, but it irritated him that he wasn't "The Most High." To be restricted in this area of his experience was more than he was prepared to tolerate, so he decided to break the bands and cords and be as God.

Today, some psychologists (and others) tell us that Christian morality is outmoded and that Christian principles are repressive. The advice they give in exchange for fat fees is "let us break their bands asunder."

Various so-called liberation movements are taking careful aim at all "repressive" institutions, and many of them say that public enemy No. 1 is the church.

Many young people have chafed at the parental control to which they have been subjected, and, because of the prevailing climate, they have been able to take to the road and head West. Their quest, of course, is the same as Lucifer's, Adam's, the kings' and rulers', the opinion makers', the frustrated husbands' and wives', and assorted other rebels' and libbers'. They look for the freedom they believe to be denied them by God's repressive requirements. They believe that if they can only rid themselves of the bands and cords, peace and joy and love will abound.

Instead, anarchy and chaos increase and growing numbers of desperate people look for answers that are not forthcoming from misguided leaders. The scene is as bleak today as when Psalm 2 was penned. Only more so!

Mud and Stars

It was Frederick Langbridge who said:

> *Two men look out through the same bars,*
> *One sees the mud and one the stars.*

He was referring to perspective of course. Downcast looks guarantee a view of mud. It takes an upward look to see the stars. Having done plenty of mud watching, the psalmist suddenly takes to star gazing. What a delightful and refreshing relief! After the heavy questions, the depressing evaluation, the sense of foreboding and hopelessness, he lifts up his eyes and reminds us that there is another perspective on this "monstrous world." The perspective of heaven.

"He that sitteth in the heavens." How easy it is to forget God! How prone even believers become to see only the horrors of their world! Some close their eyes and hope the horrors will go away. Others commit themselves to lives of sacrifice and service, endeavoring to stem the corruption and ease the pain. But whatever else happens, God must not be overlooked, because He sits "in the heavens." This expression gives a great picture of God's majestic throne, far above "the restless world that wars below." It adds a dimension to human existence without which despair is the only option left.

Laughter and Derision

But what is God doing in heaven? Why is He not intervening? The answer that the psalmist gives to those questions serves mainly to raise more questions. He *laughs*. Does that mean God derives great amusement from the pitiful children in Indochina who have known nothing but war all their short lives? Does it mean He gets slightly hysterical about bloodshed and anguish like the crowds being "entertained" by horror movies?

No! God's laughter is not from amusement or hysteria, it is derision. God has never heard anything so ludicrous as the empty boastings of man. To His ears there is nothing more inane than the arrogant rhetoric of a humanity that has repeatedly proved itself incompetent to manage its own affairs. He totally rejects any suggestion of man's that the conflict and the confusion can be resolved without reference to Him. He has no time at all for ingenious schemes that ignore His sovereignty and replace it with the sovereignty of created man. The Creator refuses to bow to the creature. He insists on the converse. The creature must acknowledge Him as Lord, and only then will peace reign in the world.

Wrath and Displeasure

We have a hard time grasping the attributes of God. Our problem is that we have only human attributes as comparisons. When we consider the love of God, we think of the most loving father we ever saw and attribute his characteristics to God. This, no doubt, helps in our understanding of God, but how are we to understand God's wrath and displeasure? Do we think of the most angry father we have ever encountered?

Does God raise His voice, get red in the face, allow His own feelings to cloud His objectivity, and sometimes lose control?

The wrath of God is as pure as the holiness of God. It is as consistent with the being of God as is His love. When God is angry He is perfectly angry. When He is displeased there is every reason that He should be, and if He were not, He would be less than perfect. His wrath and His displeasure are absolute necessities to the perfection of God.

We tend to think of anger as sin. But sometimes it is sinful *not* to be angry. If I do something wrong and am accused of the wrongdoing, I may become very angry. That anger would be simply adding sin to sin. But if I see someone abused and maltreated and instead of going to his aid, angry at his being abused, I walk away, then my lack of anger is sin.

It is unthinkable that God would not be purely and perfectly angry with sin. If He failed to deal judiciously with sin in righteous anger, we could never again be sure that wrong will ultimately be punished and right rewarded. And if we stop believing that, we immediately become dyed-in-the-wool cynics.

"My King on My Hill"

Fortunately God does not sit on His throne seething in silence. He speaks, and this is what He says, "Yet have I set My King upon My holy hill of Zion." The contrast between the kings who *set themselves* and the King whom God *has set* must not be missed. Self-exalted men will be abased. The One who humbled Himself will be exalted. The New Testament identifies this King as Christ, as any careful reader of Hebrews 1 and Paul's sermon recorded in Acts 13 knows. The King is the risen, ascended Lord Jesus.

Now a Word from the King

The risen Lord speaks with calm authority (vv. 7-9). He outlines His status, His expectations, and His intentions. None of these things is the product of His own planning and campaigning. The Father has given them to Him. It is the Father who has promised Him the nations as His inheritance. It is the Father's intention that their rebellion should be smashed and that they should be brought into subjection to the King.

The view from heaven, accordingly, yields a very striking perspective. While chaos reigns on earth as the result of man's arrogant rejection of God and man's fumbling attempts to bring his own rebellion and independence to heel, Jehovah and His Anointed One are seated in the heavens confident and competent.

Pause for Reflection

Do you remember the two men looking through the prison bars? One saw mud and the other saw stars? I get worried about both classes of people represented by these two men. The muddy-eyed pessimists and the starry-eyed optimists are both off course. What is a realistic viewpoint of our world situation? It is to be a wide-eyed realist. The realist sees earth in the light of heaven, man in the light of God, mud in the light of stars, and human impotence in the light of divine triumph. It is the great privilege of the believer to have the advantage of this realistic perspective. But like all privileges, this one brings a great responsibility.

"Be Wise Now, Therefore"

The psalmist, who started by asking questions, concludes by giving instructions. Having some answers, he knows that the answers should be shared. Having the view of heaven to add to his view of earth, he knows that he must bring the heaven view to earth and endeavor to lift the earthbound to heaven. His ministry is to lift mud to stars and bring stars to the mud. He still stands in the mud but he reaches to the stars.

His ministry is that of all who have a broad realistic understanding of the situation.

"Be wise now, therefore . . . be instructed." Notice carefully that the psalmist feels perfectly free to demand that those who have been in arrogant rebellion against God now take time out to gain some fresh knowledge. He insists that they exercise their minds. They must start thinking seriously about God's role in the affairs of men. But before any of us can insist that people exercise their minds, we must be equipped to give them an intelligent presentation of the message of Jehovah and His Anointed.

"Serve the LORD"

The message to the rebellious really begins to warm up at this point. Not only does the messenger insist that they exercise their minds but now he demands that they exert their wills: "Serve the LORD with fear, and rejoice with trembling" (v. 11). Note the words, *serve, fear, LORD, trembling.* All of them have strong emphasis on the necessity for submission and reverence, which are two of the things for which the kings were not noted.

That's how it is. If there is to be any change in the world situation, there must be a change of heart toward the Lord. That change comes only when those who have understood the truth of God submit to the claims of God in their lives.

There is a strange paradox in this experience in that submission to the Lord "in fear and trembling" brings "rejoicing." Few people object to true joy, but most of them don't realize that it comes from respectful, reverential commitment to the Lord.

"Kiss the Son"

A kiss can be both an expression of love and an acknowledgment of submission in the Old Testament. The requirement is that those who desire to serve the Lord express their feelings. They should be satisfied that He is Lord, submit to Him as Lord, and then feel very honored to be able to express this conviction openly.

Imagine the change that comes about when a former rebel, who took every opportunity to kick the Son, turns right around and publicly kisses the Son. Those who have followed his lead are confronted with a new dimension, a fresh lead, and the challenge to evaluate this change is unavoidable.

So the privileges and responsibilities of the believer are clearly spelled out. Aware of earth's turmoil and heaven's splendor, he should, fearlessly and conscientiously, alert his world to both, knowing that God has said "Blessed are all they that put their trust in Him."

Psalm 8

O LORD our Lord, how excellent is Thy name in all the earth! who hast set Thy glory above the heavens. Out of the mouth of babes and sucklings hast Thou ordained strength because of Thine enemies, that Thou mightest still the enemy and the avenger.

When I consider Thy heavens, the work of Thy fingers, the moon and the stars, which Thou hast ordained; what is man, that Thou art mindful of him? and the son of man, that Thou visitest him? For Thou hast made him a little lower than the angels, and hast crowned him with glory and honor.

Thou madest him to have dominion over the works of Thy hands; Thou hast put all things under his feet: all sheep and oxen, yea, and the beasts of the field; the fowl of the air, and the fish of the sea, and whatsoever passeth through the paths of the seas.

O LORD our Lord, how excellent is Thy name in all the earth!

3

When You Don't Like Being Human

One memorable day I had lunch in England and preached twice in California. Quite a day! I was greatly assisted by Pan American Airlines, whose flight from London to Los Angeles went nonstop over the North Pole. The ice cap is a vast area of white wilderness, unspoiled and unknown, inhabited by polar bears and seals. As far as the eye can see it glistens in severe natural starkness.

As the plane heads south, the ice gives way to tundra. Still wilderness, but not quite so formidable. After the bleak landscape of ice and snow, devoid of human habitation, it comes as a shock to see a straight and narrow road heading through the tundra to a tiny outpost.

The tundra imperceptibly gives way to prairie, the flat breadbasket of the continent. Here the signs of human intervention in the affairs of nature are to be seen on every hand. The acres of cultivation are marked by different colors according to the stage of growth and harvesting of the crops.

Prairie gives way to mountains, which give shelter to fertile valleys full of neat orderly vineyards and orange groves. Lean tall straight buildings and concrete freeways come into view as the plane descends into Los Angeles.

That journey made me proud to be human because it graphically displayed the impact of man on his environment. But the minute the plane door opened, a different feeling flooded me as smog invaded the cabin. My eyes, throat, lungs, and nose began to react violently to the acrid fumes.

Wiping my eyes, I confronted a customs official who would be nobody's choice for Mr. Conviviality. After some delay I escaped his tender mercies and was whisked into a car which was to take me to my first appointment.

Within minutes we were involved in a pile-up on the Los Angeles freeway system. About a dozen cars were sent careening in every direction to the accompaniment of screaming tires and women. Fists waved, epithets flew, sirens blared, and lights flashed —and I added tattered nerves and a throbbing headache to my smarting eyes and running nose.

These aspects of man's impact on his environment left me more ashamed than proud!

Isn't that the essence of the mystery of mankind? On the one hand humanity is so unbelievably resourceful and skilled, and on the other so crude and objectionable. He can tame the wilds but not his temper. He drills for the oil he needs from beneath the frozen wastes, but then fills the air he breathes with fumes from the oil he burns.

No wonder the philosophers of the ages have been asking, "What is man?" For any thinking person knows that today's world is what it is, not because of the giraffes or the bees but because of man. Man is the enigma of our world and without an answer to the "What is man?" question, there is little hope of answers to the world's problems.

Who Is God?

David waxed philosophical one night when he had some time on his hands. He asked the question, "What is man?" (Ps. 8:4) But note that he asked it in a different context from that in which most philosophers ask it. His question came after he had been considering not man but God (vv. 1-3). He did not make the popular mistake of starting with man in his effort to understand man. He started with God and accordingly saw man in his correct perspective.

The thinker who starts with man has nowhere else to go but

man. The one who starts with God has the opportunity to see that all things fit into a divine pattern. All things including man! So let us do what the psalmist did, and ask the question in the correct context. Let's start with God in our efforts to understand man.

"How Excellent Is Thy Name"

"O LORD our Lord" is not repetition. The first LORD is the name of Jehovah, the second Lord is His title. Like William the Conqueror or President Lincoln, "LORD Lord" speaks of name and title, and both are excellent.

As we have already seen, LORD means Jehovah, the self-existent One, and in this very name lies a great clue to the meaning of humanity. For despite what humanistic thinkers would have us believe, man is not self-sufficient. He cannot claim to have all the answers and he is not the final authority. The LORD alone is all these things and, therefore, any theory of man that starts anywhere else than with the LORD must be erroneous.

Lord, the title of Jehovah, is excellent too. It means Master. So once again, we are thrust into the position of acknowledging one Master high over all, rather than innumerable human masters who feel that they are invincible and infallible.

Much human reasoning resists these principles, of course, but I can't understand why. Personally, if I were a humanist and could see what a mess man has made, I would be thrilled to hear of an alternative to human bungling. But strangely, this is not the case. Many opponents of the LORD our Lord, soldier on, bravely and hopelessly endeavoring to salvage humanity from the ruinous products of our own ingenuity.

"Glory Above the Heavens"

Another problem with man is that he tends to be desperately earthbound in his thinking. He feels that he carries all the problems of the world on his shoulders because there aren't any other shoulders. He feels that all the answers have to come from the surface of earth because there aren't any other places from which they could be expected. Many men have little concept of the miraculous, no idea of the supernatural other than vague superstition and arms-length interest in such things as ESP, and no expectation whatsoever of the superhuman intervention of God in the affairs of men.

But how wrong can man get? Jehovah our Lord has glory that fills the heavens. He has riches of being that boggle the mind and beggar description. How puny, therefore, is the philosophy of man that ties itself to human resources and denies itself the possibility of glory from above the heavens!

Strength from Babes

Our great God is very direct in His dealings with man. "Out of the mouth of babes and sucklings" He ordains strength.

There is something deliciously uncomplicated about the way children let you know what they think and how they feel. Sucklings can't say much but they communicate most effectively. They may be suffering from not enough moisture at one end, too much at the other, or wind in between. So if you pour it in, mop it up, or burp it out, peace will reign.

God, through the "mouths of babes," is letting us know that things are basically simple and should be dealt with accordingly. Sad to say as the years go by, babes and sucklings tend to learn how to be more sophisticated and complicated. They learn how to produce neuroses, psychoses, and thromboses. In fact, the more one sees how adept people are at fouling up their lives, the more one wishes they could stay as fresh and as uncomplicated as they once were.

If only man would stop getting so smart, so sophisticated, and so enthralled with his own undeniable abilities, he might be able to save himself a lot of trouble. If only he could hear the truth of God in simple terms instead of relying on the error of man pronounced with erudition, things would be so much better.

Many a prominent executive hears more sense spoken by his own five-year-old son or daughter in prayer at bedtime than he hears all day from the men he is paying to advise him. Not that the five-year-old understands the intricacies of high finance, but he or she certainly knows enough to grasp the necessity of simple faith. To sophisticated men God speaks, "ordaining strength" through the mouth of a babe, but such men are usually preoccupied with "important" things and tend to dismiss the event with a kiss and "that's cute, honey."

"Still the Enemy"

God has His enemies and they are the enemies of mankind too. Unfortunately, man has been fooled into thinking that his worst enemies are not real. As a result he is basically defenseless against them. Nevertheless, God has His way of dealing with His enemies, and it is not man's way. He uses the foolish things to confound the wise (see 1 Cor. 1:27), or He brings power from babes to "still . . . the avenger."

Now, if man doesn't recognize the reality of God's enemies, there is no way that he will accept God's unlikely methods of defeating them. Once again we see that from the divine perspective man has things all wrong.

"When I Consider Thy Heavens"

All through history man has gazed at the heavens. Sometimes he has gotten into trouble, as Galileo did. Other times he has derived great insight as the Magi did.

In recent days, however, man has set his sights on the heavens in a new way. With consummate skill and courage, he has begun exploring the heavens. He has accepted the challenge of space. Politically, scientifically, economically, and occasionally spiritually he has explored the heavens that have enthralled him so long.

The first American astronaut came back believing in God more than when he took off. Ironically, the first Russian cosmonaut came back more convinced in the non-existence of God than when he left. The reverent soul of the astronaut saw order and beauty and attributed both to an orderly, beautiful God. The cosmonaut didn't expect to find God up there and was neither surprised nor disappointed that he didn't see Him.

Both men, of course, were acting on presuppositions. But one of those presuppositions is wrong. It must be said that if the believer in God is wrong he has lost nothing, but if the unbeliever is wrong he has lost everything!

When the psalmist looked at the heavens, he didn't do so to bolster his presuppositions; he was moved to questions. His reverent soul humbly asked, "When I consider Thy heavens . . . what is man that Thou art mindful of him?"

I like this approach to the "What is man?" question. It has content and humility and approaches the problem of man with a deep sense of wonder and reverence. The question is asked in the context of the universe as a whole and the Creator as the One who has the answer.

When the great philosophical question is asked this way, it can be answered. Asked any other way, it will never be answered.

"Thou Hast Made Him"

For years, many of our best brains have contended that man is the chance product of circumstances in a universe that is itself the freak result of unknown occurrences. This view has been particularly popular among those who find it hard or uncomfortable to believe in God. They have been able to free themselves from religious concepts and systems of morality and to produce their own substitutes. Their life-styles have reflected these substitute standards and in most instances have proved extremely attractive to contemporary society.

There is one problem, however, that unbelieving men have been unable to avoid. While it is refreshing and liberating to many people to be free of God (to believe that man has made God in his own image and that He can accordingly be dismissed with impunity), it is dehumanizing to believe that man is not a logical entity with a rational base. It is humiliating to be convinced that man is an accident and of little importance. But the theories that lead man to believe that he "just happened" also logically lead man to believe that he is meaningless. And that is dehumanizing.

But there is nothing dehumanizing about the psalmist's understanding of man. "Thou hast made him" is his great conviction.

Despite all the harsh attacks that have been made on the biblical view of man, it must be stated quite firmly that nowhere else is such a high view of man taught. From no other source will man ever gain the impression that he is anything more than a puzzle living in the middle of a muddle. But the Bible insists that man is the intelligent product of an intelligent Creator.

"A Little Lower Than the Angels"

Not only does this psalm reveal that man is made by God but it also teaches the position of the human species in the whole order of creation. "Slightly lower than the angels" is a whole lot better than slightly higher than the apes. Let's get the order straight. God, angelic beings, man, animals, and vegetables.

Obviously, the major sphere of operation for both God and the angelic beings is the heavens. There is much that we do not understand about spiritual forces, both benevolent and malevolent, but we know that they exist. There is much that we cannot grasp about the "heavenlies," but we know that such spheres of being and activity are real.

However, we do understand man and the earth, and we now know that man's role on earth is very similar and only slightly inferior to the angels. Angels are "ministering spirits" (Heb. 1:14) who serve in dimensions that are beyond human limitations, and man is a ministering spirit in the dimensions where he is equipped. God made him a little lower than the angels for this very purpose. So he functions on earth as angels operate in heaven.

"With Glory and Honor"

If man feels peeved that he was made a little lower than some other created beings, he can soon cheer up when he remembers that in his own sphere, earth, he has no equal. Here he is the pinnacle of divine creation, the one made to exhibit great glory and receive great honor. The unique glory of man is that he was made "in the image of God," specially equipped in body, soul, and spirit to know and be known of God.

There has always been a special place in the heart of God for man, whom He made superior to any other part of His earthly creation. God has shown all down the ages that He delights in man as He delights in no other part of His workmanship. God has made it possible to have the kind of fellowship with man that He has with nothing and no one else.

Man is so "fearfully and wonderfully made." He had to be made that way to be equipped for divine fellowship. It takes a mind that can understand something of the immensity of God, a heart that will respond to what the mind has grasped, and a will that can acknowledge in action what the mind grasped and the heart felt. Intellectually honored, emotionally glorious, and volitionally unique, man is truly "crowned with glory and honor."

"To Have Dominion"

If man has been made supreme in the earthly realm and gifted uniquely for a special relationship with his Creator, it is no surprise to discover that God has given man a superb role in His plan. It is to have dominion over all the works of [God's] hands."

The psalmist limits his list of the works of God's hands to various strata of animal life, but we must not assume that man's mandate is limited to these areas for he goes on to say, "[God] has put all things under his feet."

It is hard for us to know exactly what happened in the beginning. We will never know this side of heaven exactly what God did, how He did it, how long He took, what methods He used. It is unlikely that we will ever harmonize, adequately, our discoveries in the scientific realm with the statements of theologians.

Nevertheless, some things are quite clear. One clear fact is that God made a fantastic world and set man loose in it to develop and explore it. Man's unbelievable mandate was to use his God-given talent to discover the resources of earth and to adapt all that he found to the development of God's creation in every sphere. What a challange to man's creativity and ingenuity! And what a remarkable job man has done!

At some point in antiquity, he took a round stone, stuck a stake through it, sat his wife on top, and the original Cadillac was born. Man began to build roads and bridges and dams, houses and cities, ships and cars. He explored the wildernesses and found coal and oil and iron and salt. He made contact lenses and laser beams and televisions and SSTs. He found cures for tuberculosis and vaccines for polio. He opened hearts and transplanted kidneys, made music and painted pictures.

Man has come a long way from the day when God made him to have dominion. In fact, he subdued everything in the world and then headed for space, looking for other worlds to conquer. That is, he subdued everything but one. He never did learn to subdue himself. And therein lies the root of the human dilemma.

The Errant King

It is regrettable that man is the arch-producer and arch-polluter. He manufactures scalpels and submarines. He heals and harms, educates and exterminates. He can overflow with humanitarian goodwill and then explode in inhumanity to man. At the office he can be the essence of civility to his client and at home the ultimate in boorishness to his wife.

It is an undeniable fact that without man, this world would be infinitely better and infinitely worse. Infinitely better because without man there would be no war and no divorce and no heartache. If there were no human beings, there would be no pollution and no crime. There would be only clear streams, wide open horizons, virgin forests, and natural development.

But without man the world would be infinitely worse because there would be no art or music or literature. There never would have been the joy of a newborn baby's cry, the thrill of a wedding, the glow of love. Minerals would lie hidden forever in the earth, oil untapped, and coral reefs unknown. Diamonds would never have been cut to reflect a thousand sparkles. There would be no language or printing or books or verse. There would have been no cathedrals with soaring arches and no one to capture majestic sunsets on film. It would be an odd world without man.

Man is both the golden boy and the black sheep of our world. He is the unquestioned master of all the earth's resources and the undoubted mastermind behind many of the world's ills. So any discussion of the great question, "What is man?" must take this into account.

It must be admitted that the psalm before us does not develop this line of thought. However, the Bible does. At some point something got into the golden boy that made him the black sheep. There is enough of good and brilliance in the human race to convince an honest person that man was made in the image of God. However, there are many things about man that would lead the same person to believe that God would resent being held responsible for much that goes to make up man. The image of God is discernible but it's a broken image, a distorted reflection.

The Fall

To my mind there is no adequate explanation for the puzzle of the human race other than in the biblical teaching of a race, made in the perfection of God for the glory of God, that rejected its calling and fell into something sadly inferior.

Any theory of chance development must fall on hard times when it is confronted with the obvious facts of man's uniqueness and unquestioned superiority over anything else in the world. With the most conciliatory attitude, it's hard to see how anyone can really put the inventor of a computer in the same class as a dolphin whose major claim to brilliance is the ability to perform pleasing antics for vacationing crowds in shirt sleeves. Chimps can certainly peel bananas with dexterity, but does that really put them in the same class with brain surgeons? Chimps and dolphins aren't in man's class when it comes to ingenuity and skill, but that isn't all bad because it means they can never manipulate the masses in a Watergate or manufacture a Gulag Archipelago. They may not have man's skill, but they don't have his evil propensities either.

There is something about man that isn't found in animals. It's called evil genius. It takes a Fall to produce a human race that retains some vestiges of God-given grandeur and at the same time demonstrates callous indifference, gross abuse, frightening fierceness, and cold calculating hate.

Can Anything Be Done about Man?

The answer to the human dilemma comes from the New Testament use of the psalm we are considering. "But we see Jesus, who was made a little lower than the angels for the suffering of death, crowned with glory and honor" (Heb. 2:9). The point of this statement is that the Lord from glory, our Lord Jesus, was for a little while made lower than the angels (He took human form) for the express purpose of tasting "death for every man." But why was this necessary? In order that "through death He might destroy him that had the power of death, that is, the devil; and deliver them who through fear of death were all their lifetime subject to bondage" (Heb. 2:14-15). There's the clue. Man, the great and glorious king of his world is in bondage to "him that [has] the power of death, . . . the devil."

So the picture is clear. Man, made in the image of God to rule and reign as the divine agent in charge of earth, rejected his place and exposed himself to the devil. The devil took brilliant man and began to manipulate him, and through him the world, not to the glory of God and the good of man, but to the glory of the devil and the ultimate destruction of both men and world. But Jesus came and through His death and resurrection dealt the devil a body blow and offered freedom from the devil's domination to all who will acknowledge Him and reject the devil.

Deliverance from the devil means considerably more than eventual bliss in heaven. It is much more than the proverbial "pie in the sky when you die." It has to do with men being free from the devil's influence to such a degree that they can become more like the people they were initially created to be. Free to subdue the earth for the purpose of God rather than the greed of man. Librated from devilish dynamics and brought under the power of divine principle.

Bringing Sons to Glory
So where is it all going to end? Many sons are going to be brought to glory (see Heb. 2:10). Consider this one thought. If human beings with such undeniable potential for good can be released from evil and brought under the benevolent control of the Lord, who then starts leading them nearer and nearer to glory, isn't there a possibility of a deep and full and meaningful life for millions? And if that is so, shouldn't more of us give more time and effort to teaching human beings what they can be in Christ?

Psalm 11

In the Lord put I my trust: how say ye to my soul, "Flee as a bird to your mountain?" For, lo, the wicked bend their bow, they make ready their arrow upon the string, that they may privily shoot at the upright in heart. If the foundations be destroyed, what can the righteous do?

The Lord is in His holy temple, the Lord's throne is in heaven. His eyes behold, His eyelids try, the children of men.

The Lord trieth the righteous: but the wicked and him that loveth violence His soul hateth. Upon the wicked He shall rain snares, fire and brimstone, and an horrible tempest: this shall be the portion of their cup.

For the righteous Lord loveth righteousness; His countenance doth behold the upright.

4

When All You Know Is Discouragement

Bumper stickers sometimes convey messages that are implicitly contradicted by those driving the cars on which they are displayed. One night when I was driving in the pouring rain, I was almost run off the road by a car that passed me where there was no room to pass. Through my rain-covered windshield, I was just able to decipher the bumper sticker: "See you in church on Sunday."

Another day I was exhorted to "Honk if you love Jesus" by the bumper sticker on the car ahead of me at the traffic lights. So I did, and the driver turned around and shook his fist at me!

A recent cartoon in a national magazine showed a little man in a car whose sticker read "Honk if you believe in anything." He represents a lot of people in our world who are downright despondent and discouraged.

No doubt there is much to make people discouraged. But there is no reason why anyone should stay discouraged. There are many good answers to discouragement and some of them are to be found in Psalm 11. David had plenty of practice coping with discouraging situations and gave us the benefit of his experience.

"Flee as a Bird to Your Mountain"

At times David was in such a tight corner that discretion rather than valor would appear to have been the wisest course. His situation was not helped by a group of anonymous advisers who suggested that, as the situation was hopeless, he should pack his bags and run for his life. In all probability he had been tempted to think that way himself.

Not long ago a youngster was brought into my office just as I was about to go into the Sunday evening service. The kids who brought him said he was taking off for Texas and wondered if I could make an announcement in the church to see if anyone was going in his direction and would give him a ride. I pointed out to them that the possibilities of someone leaving Wisconsin for Texas on a Sunday night were remote but I would be happy to help him in some other way if possible. As I talked with him, his story came tumbling out: parents divorced, mother remarried, stepfather belligerent, conflict at home, his school work suffering, trouble at school, assignments missed, dropping out of school, getting a job, becoming unemployed, and, finally, running away. And he was only 16 at this time.

People have a natural tendency to flee to the mountains when things get tough. And it isn't only young people who feel this way. Not infrequently my phone rings late at night. Usually the call is from a potential suicide or an alcoholic. Either way, the person concerned is fleeing to his or her mountain. Reality for him has become too much, and a flight from reality is the only alternative he sees open to him.

"The Wicked Bend Their Bow"

David's "encouragers" went on to point out that there were some people out to get him. I don't suppose that this fact had escaped his attention. When the arrows start falling around you thick and fast, you do tend to get the impression you are being used for target practice. And you do have a reflex reaction to run for cover. But running for cover and running from the field altogether are entirely different.

Sometimes circumstances pile in on people to such an extent that it seems there's no end to what can happen. Two weeks ago a young wife and mother in our congregation was rushed into the hospital because a lump had suddenly appeared in her throat. Malignancy was in everyone's mind. Emergency surgery followed. The tumor was removed and shown to be benign. Great relief was theirs until their six-week-old baby started to run temperatures of 105°. Meningitis was the diagnosis, and once again the young parents were under pressure. All this came after severe problems in other areas relating to work and family. Things can get tough, and the tougher things get, the harder it is to resist discouragement.

Destroyed Foundations

It is difficult to say which foundations David's advisers meant when they said, "If the foundations be destroyed, what can the righteous do" (v. 3). Whenever foundations of any kind are destroyed, the result can be that horrid sinking feeling.

There are those who believe that the foundations of our contemporary society are being destroyed:

- The honorable foundations of integrity, honesty and moral and ethical standards
- The principle of "a fair day's pay for a fair day's work"
- Respect for the sanctity and permanence of marriage and the necessity of a stable family and home

As a result, many people quite understandably think that our society is sinking because our foundations are crumbling. And I for one am not about to disagree on that point.

But what do many of these people do? They flee as a bird to their mountain. They quit. They cop out. They decide that they will concentrate on protecting themselves in the midst of inevitable disintegration. They write off their society and yield to their fear and discouragement.

"What can the righteous do?" I get the impression that this question was asked with a note of pathetic defeat. Rather like Andrew's, "What are they among so many?" when all he could find was five loaves and two fishes to feed the hungry multitudes. Far be it from me to criticize Andrew or the unknown friends of David, but I believe the righteous should never quit. I have a firm conviction that, while the believer will inevitably be as open to arrows and prone to discouragement as the next man, the similarity should end there. When the discouraged flee for the mountains, Christians should take another course and talk like David.

"In the Lord Put I My Trust"

Be careful that you do not miss the point of this psalm. The psalmist is responding to the pessimistic advice he has been receiving concerning his discouraging circumstances. "How say ye to my soul, 'Flee as a bird'?" There is a note of outrage in his response.

David's words could, of course, have been words of blustering self-confidence or frightened belligerence. But in this case they are not. David speaks here with the calm voice of faith. "In the Lord put I my trust."

In the New Testament the words *faith* and *believe* are very common but in the Old Testament *trust* is the common word. In fact, it occurs over 150 times. Today, we have evolved some ideas about faith that are somewhat disturbing. To have faith or to believe is, in the thinking of many people, little more than agreeing with certain facts. So to believe or have faith in the Lord is for many people nothing more than giving assent to the facts of the Lord's existence. But the Old Testament word *trust* reminds us that there is much more to faith than intellectual assent. Real faith trusts what it believes.

My dad believed implicitly that airplanes fly. He had no alternative because he had seen them doing so on many occasions. But he was adamant about the fact that he would "never set foot in one of those contraptions." And he never did. He went to glory without the help of a plane. But he never experienced either the thrill of flying or the value of aviation. He believed, but his belief never extended to trust.

Now notice carefully that David's answer to discouragement is not believing about the Lord but putting trust in the Lord. And trusting involves a number of things.

To Take Refuge

Three different Hebrew words are translated "trust" in the psalms. In this psalm, the word means "to take refuge in." As soon as believers start talking about taking refuge in the Lord, their opponents jump for joy. "There you are," they say, "these believers have wishbones instead of backbones. They are so inadequate they have to manufacture a God to help them cope."

One thing must be said to people who talk like that. They must be made to see that *everyone is inadequate* at some point in his experience. This they cannot deny. Sooner or later, even the most self-possessed person will crumble. Tragedy, old age, sickness—there comes some point in everyone's life when he realizes he has gone as far as he can. The realistic thing to do, therefore, is to admit this and start planning for it. As soon as a person does this, he will find many other areas of inadequacy of which he may not have been aware.

We all have basic needs of such things as security. Some people more than others. We show our need for security in different ways. Some people need a secure home situation, a retreat where they can be in their own place and do their own thing. Others need to be told how much they are appreciated, how well they are doing, and how invaluable they are. Without this, they tend to fall apart. Little children drag dirty security blankets with them. Many business executives appear to need opulent offices or status symbol limousines.

In addition to security needs of this nature, we have real need of security in the area of the spirit. When it comes to coping with sickness of soul, limousines and expensive drapes are of no more use than security blankets. There has to be some place of refuge to which the overextended one can go. There has to be a Lord in whom refuge can be found.

People tell me that I give the impression of coping quite well with pressures and problems. Some say that they won't come to me for advice because either I don't have problems or apparently I cope with them so effectively that they would feel stupid coming to me. The fact of the matter is that I take refuge in the Lord. Unashamedly I run to Him. In fact, if it were not for the ready access I have to Him, I would never survive the ministry. The pressures would be more than I could take. I hide myself away with Him. I crawl into a corner and talk to Him. When the pressure is on, I pull the drapes and commune with Him. I take refuge in Him.

Leaning on the Lord
Another word translated "trust" means "to lean upon." "They

that know Thy name will put their *trust* in Thee" (Ps. 9:10). Shortly after I arrived in Milwaukee, I met with a group of young people. After I had discussed the things of God with them for some considerable time, a young lady who was sitting on the floor burst out, "I can't stand another minute of this." I thought she was referring to her uncomfortable position on the floor. But she went on, "All this talk about God is nonsense. God is the result of weak people looking for a crutch. Your God is nothing more than a crutch."

She was really hot so I chose not to interrupt. Eventually, when she appeared to be about through with her monologue, I said, "You are one of the most interesting people I have ever met. If you were skiing and broke your leg, you would be taken to the hospital and have your leg set in plaster. A man with a white coat would give you a stick of wood with a rubber cup on one end, an armpit-shaped pad on the other, and a handle in the middle. Presumably you would object violently at being given a crutch!

"Crutches are not to be despised; they are to be appreciated, because they meet needs perfectly. Anyone who admits to need, welcomes the answer to that need. You are no more against God than you are against crutches. You simply won't admit that you need support."

This is the problem for many people. Even when it is obvious that they are craving support, they deny it. They try to cover up their feelings in many ways but they must learn to admit to their need and find in the Lord One on whom they can lean. This is the life of faith, the experience of trust.

I know a man who is deeply discouraged. He tries to hide his very real problems. He endeavors to run away from his crushing load. Whenever I see him, I share the things of the Lord with him, encouraging him to lean on the Lord and to find in Him support that will be of inestimable help. But he always holds back. It isn't that he doesn't "believe." He's a firm believer that the Lord exists, but he feels that he must try to find all the solutions himself and battle the insuperable odds alone. Frankly, I fear for him as I fear for anyone who is not in a position to say, "In the Lord put I my trust."

To Roll upon

Psalm 22 is a remarkable prophetic statement concerning the crucifixion of our Lord. While on the cross in dying agony, the Lord Jesus made reference to Psalm 22 and, strangely, even His detractors quoted it too. "He trusted on the Lord that He would deliver Him" (v. 8). This word *trust* means literally "to roll upon."

The enemies of the Lord Jesus knew many things about Him, and one of them was that He "rolled Himself upon Jehovah." They didn't like that. In fact, they ridiculed Him even on the cross. While their vindictiveness comes through with startling clarity in this passage of Scripture, the fact of the Lord's relationship with the Father is even more startling.

There were situations in the life of the Lord Jesus through which He moved like no man has ever moved. The reserves of strength He exhibited and the fortitude He displayed have amazed men and women through the centuries. But never forgot how He did it. "He trusted in God."

An obvious question comes to mind. "If He needed to operate this way, what makes me think I can get by without rolling my burden on the Lord?"

One of the first stories I remember hearing from a pulpit described an old woman going to market carrying a large basket of dairy produce. A local farmer riding along to market in his "pony and trap" stopped and offered her a ride, which she gladly accepted. After a few minutes had elapsed, the farmer noticed the woman was sitting hugging her large heavy basket. When he suggested that she put it on the floor she replied, "Oh, no, thank you, I'd prefer to hold it on my knee and keep the weight off the horse."

Go on, laugh! But don't laugh too loudly because, if you are like me, you probably do the same thing with the Lord. You don't roll the burden on the Lord. But you must, if you are ever to cope with the discouragements through which you will pass and the disappointments which will be yours.

David had an alternative approach to discouragement. His reaction to despondent advice was quick and powerful. "In the Lord put I my trust: how say ye to my soul, 'Flee to your mountain'?" His trust was in God.

Who Is Trusting What?

We must not get the impression that only believers trust when things get tough. Everybody trusts something. "Some trust in chariots, and some in horses: but we will remember the name of the Lord our God" (Ps. 20:7). Everybody is trusting something but the things they trust vary considerably: *horses, chariots,* or *the name of our God.*

Tanks and missiles replace horses and chariots as objects of trust today. Many of our contemporaries are despondent about the world situation, and nations have resorted to massive arms races to try to produce some international stability. Many others trust to "luck," and even more just seem to have an inbred trust that *somebody will think of something.*

It should be obvious that not everything people trust is worthy of trust.

- Thousands trusted Hitler implicitly and were destroyed.
- Millions voted for Nixon and were disillusioned.
- Some who trust faith healers die.
- The foolish trust to luck only to find Lady Luck is cruel.

People may have great willingness to "lean on" luck or "take refuge" in tanks or "roll on" charismatic leaders, but that is no guarantee that all will be well. In fact, the very trust that they place in these things may lead to disaster, not because trust is disastrous but because they trust untrustworthy things.

This leads us to consider the most important thing about trust: its object. My dad used to tell the story of a big fat Sunday School teacher who placed a chair on the platform in full view of about 500 kids and said, "Boys and girls, I am now going to demonstrate what trust is." With that he threw his great weight on the unoffending chair, which promptly collapsed. To the unspeakable delight of the kids, he landed flat on his back amid the ruins, with his feet in the air. One scruffy kid with tears running down his face said, "This is better than the movies."

The large demonstrator of trust regained his feet and his composure, held his hands up to silence the crowd and said, "I tried to demonstrate one thing to you and managed to demonstrate two. I showed you what trust is, but I also showed you that you must be careful what you put your trust in." Exactly. David's trust was in the Lord.

The Lord Who Intercedes
The psalmist describes the Lord as being "in His holy temple" (11:4). This immediately brings to my mind a picture of the priest quietly and efficiently going about his business in the temple, offering sacrifices and prayers on behalf of the people. The Lord Jesus Christ is shown in many roles in Scripture, and His ministry as our Great High Priest is one of the most beautiful. Our ascended Lord "ever liveth to make intercession for [us]" (Heb. 7:25). That means that part of the present ministry of the Lord is to pray on our behalf.

This has a direct bearing on what a person should do when he becomes despondent. Should he flee to his mountain, or should he trust the Lord who is praying for him? The answer is quite plain. To flee is unthinkable in such circumstances. To lean upon this fact, to roll upon this High Priest, to take refuge in this temple is the way to go.

The Lord Who Reigns
Nebuchadnezzar was a dreamer who forgot what he had dreamed. But he didn't say, "It was only a dream." He sent for his professional dream interpreters and told them they would be cut in little pieces if they didn't come up with both dream and interpretation quickly.

Daniel came on the scene at this time and, like the rest of the men in his field, he was facing an "early retirement." However, instead of being understandably despondent at the situation he said, "There is a God in heaven" (Dan. 2:28) and proceeded to tackle the problem.

The story of Daniel is a great one for people who have demanding employers! It's also great for all who need to be reminded constantly that God does reign in the affairs of men. There is a throne in heaven and there is a God on that throne. Trust in the ruling One lifts the despondent and stops them from fleeing to their mountains.

The Lord Who Watches

A friend of mine told me he was putting his small boy to bed one night and after the usual, I-want-a-drink-of-water and tell-me-a-story routines, he was about to leave the room when the boy said, "Put the light on, Dad." Thinking this was a new method of stalling, my friend said, "No, go to sleep."

The youngster began to cry so the light went on and the tears dried miraculously. "I just wanted to see your face, Dad, 'cause then I can tell you love me."

This was not another delaying technique. It was a small boy saying something profound. The way we look at people or don't look at them often tells more about our attitudes than what we say. The psalmist has a magnificent thought for the despondent: "His eyes behold." There is no time when the Lord is not carefully, lovingly watching over His own.

The Lord Who Evaluates

"His eyelids try the children of men." Now there's a strange and beautiful expression. I didn't understand it until I was talking to a group of students one day about spiritual realities. They were listening intently and skeptically. Intent on my every word they had narrowed their eyes to tiny slits. Their eyelids were trying me, carefully weighing me up, evaluating, checking. Critically!

By contrast, have you ever observed a trainer watching a young boxer? He stands in the corner studying every move, every blow, waiting to see how much his youngster can take, ready to jump to his assistance at any given moment.

There are those whom the Lord views critically, as the students viewed me. His eyelids try them. There are others who know His eyelids try them not critically but lovingly. Both the righteous and the unrighteous know His searching gaze. To the one it speaks judgment but to the other, because he knows God well, loving concern.

The composite of the Lord that we now have is enough to encourage even the most despondent person to pause and reflect. But there is one final aspect of the knowledge of the Lord that we should mention.

Beholding His Countenance

Depending on which translation of the Bible you use, you may read the last verse of the psalm as "His countenance doth behold the righteous," or perhaps "the righteous will behold His countenance." Both are true of course, and either of these statements would do justice to the text.

Let's examine the second possibility. Hope is the ingredient that is missing in many a despondent person's life. But it is not missing in the trusting believer's experience because in addition to knowing he has God as High Priest and King and Judge, he knows that one day he will behold the countenance of his Lord. This is the glorious hope of the trusting soul.

So if you feel like quitting your job, leaving your wife, taking to the road, dropping out of school, transferring your membership, emigrating to another country, or moving into your bombshelter, don't! At least, not in discouragement! Hold it a minute and ask yourself the question, "Have I allowed all these things to get on top of me so much that I have forgotten to trust the Lord?" When you have asked yourself that question, try to answer it. Then decide whether you should flee as a bird to your mountain or whether you should look your discouragements straight in the eye and shout, "In the Lord put I my trust: how say ye . . . 'Flee as a bird to your mountain'?"

Psalm 19

The heavens declare the glory of God; and the firmament showeth His handiwork. Day unto day uttereth speech, and night unto night showeth knowledge. There is no speech nor language, where their voice is not heard.

Their line is gone out through all the earth, and their words to the end of the world. In them hath He set a tabernacle for the sun, which is as a bridegroom coming out of his chamber, and rejoiceth as a strong man to run a race. His going forth is from the end of the heavens, and his circuit unto the ends of it: and there is nothing hid from the heat thereof.

The law of the Lord is perfect, converting the soul; the testimony of the Lord is sure, making wise the simple. The statutes of the Lord are right, rejoicing the heart: the commandment of the Lord is pure, enlightening the eyes. The fear of the Lord is clean, enduring forever: the judgments of the Lord are true and righteous altogether. More to be desired are they than gold, yea, than much fine gold: sweeter also than honey and the honeycomb. Moreover by them is Thy servant warned: and in keeping of them there is great reward.

Who can understand his errors? Cleanse Thou me from secret faults. Keep back Thy servant also from presumptuous sins; let them not have dominion over me: then shall I be upright, and I shall be innocent from the great transgression. Let the words of my mouth, and the meditation of my heart, be acceptable in Thy sight, O Lord, my Strength, and my Redeemer.

5

When You Wonder Where to Get Answers

Sometimes I sit down and think about the fact that our world is rather ridiculous. Depending on how I feel at the time, my reaction varies from laughing to crying. Have you ever thought how silly it is that millions of us should be on a little planet spinning in space? We don't know where it's heading, we don't get along with each other, most of us have never seen much of the rest of the planet, and the majority of us don't really care about it. Just so long as we have food in our stomachs, a roof over our heads and money in our pockets, the spinning world can go its crazy way for all we care. We can't stop it spinning, we can't change its course. There's not a thing we can do about its relation to anything. We're stuck with it, and on it, except for a handful of people who have taken desperately expensive trips away for a week or two.

Thinkers
However, some people will not settle for the indifferent approach. They are unwilling to spin aimlessly in space caring nothing about why they spin. From time long past there has been a strange breed of person who loves to take long walks or sit under trees, scratching bald spots and thinking. *Philosophers* we call them. They are people who try to work out principles that lie behind human conduct and thought. They endeavor to seek out meaning and knowledge and unravel the mysteries of existence and the universe.

Fascinating people they are too! Next time you see someone with a bald spot taking a long walk, get into conversation with him. He may be one of those rare birds who thinks about things other than sex and money and sport!

You may learn something. On the other hand, you may find that he has not come up with any answers. The more he thinks, the more uncertain he may become. This is not uncommon among thinkers as is indicated by the fact that thinkers spend much of their time thinking about what other thinkers think and deciding that they think others are thinking wrong! So philosophy can be confusing and discouraging.

The problem is knowing where to start. If a clever thinker says to himself as he looks at his reflection in a pool, "There I am; at least, I think I am there," he starts with a rather shaky premise. If he goes on from there to try to understand everything around him in terms of his own being, he will end up with a system of thought which may well be brilliant but will certainly be inadequate.

There is another approach to the whole business of thought about existence and meaning. Instead of starting with the human mind trying to reach into mysteries it cannot comprehend, one may listen to God. This approach is exactly the opposite of speculation. It is called revelation. Instead of being nothing more than the product of human ingenuity (which is undoubtedly great despite its attendant limitations), revelation is the product of divine thought —eternal, infinite, limitless.

It's rather like a kid finding a transistorized calculator in a field and sitting down under a tree scratching his head and speculating about what he has found. *I think it's a bomb and if I press this button and throw it over there, I can blow up my school.* Good speculation but inaccurate.

Having tried that without success, he thinks again, *I know! It's a dictionary that fell out of a flying saucer, and if I press enough of these buttons I might learn to speak Martian.* Good speculation, but learning Martian soon proves to be as difficult and boring as learning Latin. And the calculator is no good for either!

More speculation is necessary. Unless, of course, a little man with a shabby raincoat and big glasses comes by, sees the kid, and says, "Thank goodness, you've found the calculator I lost. I've been working on that thing for years. Here let me show you what it is and how it works." That will mean the end of speculation for the boy and the beginning of revelation.

God Has Spoken

The big fly in the ointment of this approach is the question of whether God actually has spoken or will speak. And if so, will we understand His language? The clear statement of Scripture is that He has spoken, does speak, and we can understand. If this is true, it must be one of the most exciting things known to man.

If the great Creator has left some indication of what He had in mind originally and what He is doing in an ongoing way, that information must be second to none available to mankind. There are two main areas in which God has spoken in understandable language, and Psalm 19 contains information about both.

The first way God speaks is through creation. A strange voice, you may say, for created things use "no speech nor language, their voice is not heard" (as verse 3 reads in the *New American Standard Bible.*) But they speak, nevertheless, and with unrelenting force and clarity. Everyone on the face of this earth has been confronted one way or another with the silent voice of creation.

The second way God speaks is through Scripture. This is a far more detailed voice than that of creation. It speaks in specific terms where creation deals only in generalities. In fact, without the voice of Scripture, much of creation would be a complete enigma to us, but when both voices speak, they reveal the mysteries of God and earth in stereophonic force and clarity.

Here is a different approach to the search for knowledge than the speculative philosophy route. Revelation can clarify, where speculation may only mystify. Thus, it becomes clear that one of modern society's great needs is to turn once more to the revelation of God for answers rather than lean upon the speculations of man.

"The Heavens Declare"

"Red sky at night, shepherd's delight;
Red sky at morning, shepherd's warning."

Variations on this theme are known around the world. In this sense, many people accept the statement that the heavens declare. In much more sophisticated ways, meteorologists look to the heavens to declare what a day will bring forth, and this information is fed as a daily diet to millions through the media. But the psalmist has more in mind than weather forecasts. He speaks of the heavens declaring "the glory of God."

To the reverent observer, the heavens continually speak of numerous aspects of the glory of God. But I believe the heavens speak to the less reverent too. For instance, any informed observer of the heavens, reverent or not, knows that at any one time only 2,500 stars are visible to the naked eye. This number can be increased *ad infinitum* depending on the quality of the equipment used. In fact, the more we study the heavens, the more immense they appear. There is no discernible end to them.

Light years are things we get out of our system once we graduate from high school. In case you've gotten them so far out that you can't remember what a light year is, let me remind you that for some reason known only to God, light travels at the remarkable speed of 186,282 miles per second. Multiply that by 60 (seconds in a minute), then by 60 (minutes in an hour), then by 24 (hours in a day), then by 365 (days in a year) and you have the distance light travels in a year. Approximately six trillion miles. Sirius, one of our bright friends, is about 54 trillion miles away or 9 light years.

What is a person to think about all this immensity? If he will allow the heavens to speak in their immensity, I believe he will begin to think of the immensity of the Creator.

I happen to be convinced that one of the best things that we can learn from any source is that there is a great and glorious God, who has given us some little idea of His glory by letting us see something of His creative genius. I also believe that the revelation of His immensity is one of the most necessary things for our world at this time. For one thing, when people begin to realize that God is the God of the heavens, they may think twice about trying to twist Him round their little fingers. They may, on the other hand, begin to feel a little more confident about the world situation if they get a glimpse of Him as revealed in the immense heavens.

"Day unto Day"

One of the most boring things you can do is fly the Atlantic for about the thirtieth time. You may take off from the American side of the ocean late in the evening and wait about an hour and a half for something to eat while all the booze is served. Then you eat your meal and start dozing.

The movie comes on, and the captain announces that it is now 3 A.M. Greenwich Mean Time. The people next to you climb over you to pay their third visit to the rear of the aircraft, and you wait for them to return. The cabin gets cool so you hunt for a blanket and snooze fitfully until you give up and try to read. But your eyes feel as if they are full of sand so you decide to go for a walk, to the one place there is to go, only to discover that everyone else on the plane is asleep.

One thing on the trip makes all this tedium almost worthwhile: *the dawn is gorgeous.* Slowly the blackness begins to pale and a succession of pastel colors acts as an overture to the sunrise. That's one lovely thing to anticipate.

It's comforting to know that sunrise will come right on time. We reckon on it and even talk about the certainty of it: "As sure as day follows night." That's what the psalmist means when he says, "Day unto day uttereth speech." The fact that the days come and go with total consistency and reliability says something about God's fidelity and reliability. That is something else we need to know in today's world. We need to be reassured that the God of immensity is the God of fidelity.

The psalmist says that the message of the heavens reaches to "the end of the world" (v. 4). This is not referring, of course, to the climactic moment of earth's history, but to a poetic place that cannot literally exist on a globe. The point of the statement is that there is no point on the earth's surface where the message of the heavens has not been preached.

Still referring to the heavens, the psalmist goes on to say, "In them has He set a tabernacle for the sun" (v. 4). There is so much beautiful description of the sun in this psalm (vv. 4-6) that I feel reluctant to comment. Allow me to point out, however, two things on the mind of the psalmist.

First, he thinks of the freshness and exuberance of the daily sunrise and says it reminds him of a bridegroom on his wedding day. (As a pastor who has officiated at many weddings, I must say that my experience of bridegrooms has not always been so positive! But that's not important.)

Second, the sun is relentless in moving through its circuit, touching to a greater or lesser extent the ends of the earth. What a picture of radiant, irresistible, benevolent majesty, and how easy it is to apply this revelation to the being of God.

These are some of the things the heavens say to those who take time to listen to their silent message.

Before we go further, let's pause and consider the thrust of the psalm so far. The heavens declare in no uncertain terms the glory, immensity, fidelity, and majesty of God. They say it silently, but eloquently. And they say it to the ends of the earth.

But something is missing in this revelation. The picture of God we now have is remote and vast and vaguely disturbing. Is that all that God is willing to reveal of Himself? If so, a person might almost prefer not to know, rather than to be tantalized with such a frustrating partial view of God. The sheer unapproachableness and other-worldliness of God as He is revealed in the heavens does little to warm the heart of the observer, and does even less to allay his fears and instruct his mind. Man needs a further revelation.

"The Law of the Lord"

There has been a message from heaven in detailed form, and it fills in many of the blanks left by the creation revelation. This remarkable revelation of God is the inspired Scriptures. At this point we must say a fond but firm farewell to much of man's philosophy, for human thinking and scriptural truth seldom equate in our day (if they ever did). Accordingly, people have to decide to which they will listen and upon which they will build their lives.

Scriptural truth has fallen on deaf ears in most areas of contemporary society. Much of what people think today about the mysteries of life comes not from God and His scriptural revelation, but from man and his limited and often erroneous speculation. To put it bluntly, we have an awful lot of dangerous nonsense filling the areas of people's minds that were intended for the truth of God as revealed in Scripture.

Without laboring the point, let me offer one example. There is so much thinking today on the subject of "rights." Many of society's problems at this time appear to be caused by people's rights being abused and by the resultant reaction of those who have been abused. As a result, we are almost totally "rights" oriented.

The Scriptures, however, speak far more about responsibilities than rights. This means that if people concentrated on their responsibilities, others would have their rights.

But in all honesty, do you think there will come a day when people will stop insisting on their rights and start persisting in their responsibilities? I have tried this theory on a number of people and they all look at me with a degree of incredulity. "You've gotta be kidding," they say. Yet I insist that unless we return to scriptural principle and throw out much that is the product of humanistic thought, we have our course set straight for societal shipwreck.

What God's Word Will Do for You
On warm Sunday mornings when the golf course beckons, there is sometimes a conflict as to where people will look for divine revelation. "I can worship God on the golf course as readily as in church," some say.

I for one do not dispute that. I simply ask, "Do you?"

The fact of the matter is that in a good church one will hear the word of God proclaimed, but there is little chance of that at even the best equipped country club!

Suppose that a worshiper on a golf course worshiped the God that he saw revealed in greens and sand traps. Do you realize that he would never learn from that worship experience that his soul can be converted? They don't display that information on the tees or print it on the backs of scorecards. The Gospel's source is in the Word of God, and nowhere else.

"Making Wise the Simple"
We need to make a clear distinction between knowledge and wisdom. Knowledge is the amassing of facts. Wisdom is knowing what

on earth to do with what we've amassed. This distinction can help us understand why some remarkable, erudite people are in such quandaries and why some relatively ignorant people have peace of mind and demonstrate integrated living.

The Scriptures make simple people wise to what they should do with their knowledge. The principle is: "The fear of the Lord is the beginning of wisdom" (Ps. 111:10). Only Scripture insists on that point.

The knowledge of high finance may lead a man to make a fortune by the time he's 30, but in the making of it he may unmake his family, his health, and his integrity. If somehow or other this brilliant man could have gotten some wisdom with his knowledge, he might have acknowledged the Lord in his family relation, his use of time and energy, and in moral principles. But he would need to act on the basis of sound scriptural truth rather than on everyday businessman's ethics.

"Rejoicing the Heart"

In the first chapter of this book, we talked about the pursuit of happiness, and there is no need to say again what was said there. But remember that the way to happiness as revealed in Scripture is not heavily traveled. The biblical approach is written off by the majority of our fellow travelers as antiquated and Victorian without holding anything remotely attractive to them.

"Enlightening the Eyes"

Have you ever seen a child at his first birthday party? Do you remember how his eyes got big as saucers when he saw the cake with its one proud candle? Can you recollect the wonder of it all, the sheer thrill of the little guy? His eyes were opened to something new and strange and totally captivating.

I remember meeting a man with a Ph.D. who had just discovered the Bible. He had the same look of wonder on his face as a child with a birthday cake. He kept saying, "I didn't know that. I didn't know that." In fact, he hadn't known much, though he was about as educated (or schooled!) as one can get. But what a difference the revelation of God made in his life.

We have described only some of the things that exposure to the Word of God produces in lives. And remember that these things do not come from speculation, and only partially from the revelation of creation. It's the law of the Lord that does the trick.

"The Testimony of the Lord"

Not only are the Scriptures referred to as *law,* but also as *testimony, statutes, commandments, fear, judgments.* These terms have an authoritative ring to them which must not be overlooked. When God speaks in Scripture, He says what needs to be said and He says it as if He means it.

In many areas of society, people are looking for an authoritative leader with an authoritative voice who can tell them what to do and how to do it. In fact, we live in such a turbulent age that if someone can dream up a wild enough idea and project it with enough confidence, he almost seems guaranteed a following. Deep in the human heart, there is a great need for clear direction.

The Scriptures provide us direction without equivocation. But this in itself poses a problem because most human beings are a bundle of contradictions. They want an authoritative statement just so long as it tells them with authority that it is OK to do what they intend to do! Like the church that was looking for a pastor who would in a fearless, forthright, and uncompromising manner tell them what they wanted to hear without holding back anything!

God does not work that way. He spells things out, explains what to do, what not to do, and how to do it or not do it as the case may be. He then promises what will happen and leaves the choice to the individual. Whether you feel inclined to obey or disinclined to obey, you can be equally sure of what will happen. God has spoken.

Sure, Pure, and Right

What lovely words are used to describe the authoritative statements of Scripture. The assurance of Scripture's power and validity is the greatest possible incentive to obedience. It, more than anything else, stimulates the desire to depend upon the promises of God.

Just to know that you will be doing the *right* thing is wonderful. To be convinced that you are being told the sure, pure truth is more comforting than words can tell. It makes a person respond with great joy and confidence, "for the testimony of the Lord is sure . . . the statutes of the Lord are right . . . the commandment of the Lord is pure." This is the way to go.

Sweeter than Honey

The first time I ate a mango was an unforgettable moment. I had been told by my Jamaican friends that the only way to eat a mango is to stand up to your neck in the Caribbean. I was not particularly impressed by my first sight of a mango, but the feel of the Caribbean was just what I needed. So I waded out in the unbelievably warm water and was duly given a dry looking piece of fruit, most unappetizing in appearance. I watched how my friends got into it, did the same, and, oh, the bliss! It was just about the sweetest thing I ever tasted. I don't know if there are such people as mangoholics but if there are, I'm one of them.

Did you ever get into the dry, dull pages of the revealed truth of God in Scripture and taste the sweetness? Did you come to its pages with fear and find sweet peace? Have you come with guilt and found sweet forgiveness? This is the beauty of the Word of God. It is sweeter than honey (v. 10). If you obey it and believe it, then that which is authoritative becomes attractive. Fight and resist it, and it becomes unbelievably bitter.

Warning and Reward

The strange and wonderful book that God has given to us is not only authoritative and attractive but it manages to be abrasive too. "Moreover by them is Thy servant warned, and in keeping of them there is great reward" (v. 11). This is straight talking, and there is no doubt that Scripture is a little too hot for some to handle. But there's one thing to remember about abrasive materials. If you let them rub with the grain, they smooth things out, but if you rub against the grain, they rough things up. It all depends on the reaction of the material being abraded!

This leads us to the final section of the psalm (vv. 12-14), in which the writer shows something of the response of his own heart to the truths God has revealed to him.

"Cleanse Me"

The Word of God functions in many ways. Sometimes it comes on like a trumpet; other times it hits like a hammer. Then it acts like a seed quietly growing in the soil of the hearer's heart.

David sees the Scripture more as a mirror as ne comes to the conclusion of this psalm. The Word of God has made him conscious of his own errors of judgment and action. He seeks forgiveness. He has also seen the cover stripped away from his "secret sins." He wants to be clean of this kind of behavior. Then he has been made painfully aware that some of his living has been downright disobedience. He calls it "presumptuous sin," and his great desire is to be freed from the tyranny that he experiences in this area.

This is the kind of response that the Lord expects from the person who hears the Word of God and allows it to sink deep into his heart. The response is totally different from that of the person who is still working on the basis of speculation. He tends to operate on procedures that seem right, but if they don't work out, he speculates again and comes up with something else—that also doesn't work.

The approach of the natural man is as unsatisfactory as a referee changing rules half way through a game rather than sticking with the rules and enforcing them. Rules enforced lead to a completed game. Rules ignored or changed lead to chaos.

The challenge of living according to what God has said, rather than vacillating around what man has thought, is one of the greatest of all challenges. It leads to a reevaluation of the words that come from the lips and even a careful look at the very thoughts that churn in the mind. And the real push comes when, having taken note of these things, the person concerned says, "Let the words of my mouth and the meditation of my heart be acceptable in Thy sight, O Lord" (v. 14).

Instead of a variety of theories emanating from a host of philosophies which breed inevitable conflicts of thought and ideology, this approach leads to great unity of purpose: the desire to please God according to His revealed will. There's hope in this approach; there's none in the other.

Psalm 23

The Lord is my shepherd; I shall not want. He maketh me to lie down in green pastures: He leadeth me beside the still waters. He restoreth my soul: He leadeth me in the paths of righteousness for His name's sake.

Yea, though I walk through the valley of the shadow of death, I will fear no evil: for Thou art with me; Thy rod and Thy staff they comfort me. Thou preparest a table before me in the presence of mine enemies: Thou anointest my head with oil; my cup runneth over.

Surely goodness and mercy shall follow me all the days of my life: and I will dwell in the house of the Lord forever.

6

When You Don't Know Who or What You Are

I know a woman who has spent years concentrating on the fact that she is a failure. According to her, everything she has tried in the past has failed, and there is no possibility of her ever being able to succeed at anything in the future. She has made a number of "attempts" at suicide and has even failed in these. Her children are suffering, her husband is suffering, her marriage has suffered, and just about everything has fallen apart because of her poor self-image.

On the other hand, there are people who seem to have an inflated self-image that leaves others almost gasping in disbelief.

Many women, feeling that they have been oppressed, are marching on the bastions of masculine supremacy chanting,

"I am woman; I am invincible . . . ."

Far be it from me to dispute the fact that many women have had a raw deal. And I would certainly not deny that many women have been living far below capacity because of masculine obduracy. Neither would I overlook the fact that mobilized women are a force to be reckoned with. I agree with William Congreve, "Hell hath no fury like a woman scorned." But invincible? No, ladies, I can't go along with that. And that's realism, not chauvinism! To be thinking and talking about invincibility is to lay oneself open to disaster, because it projects as inaccurate a self-image as the "total failure" person projects.

Robert Burns, the Scottish poet mused,
 Oh wad some Power the giftie gie us
 To see oursels as ithers see us.
That kind of talking is healthy. One of the best antidotes to a
faulty self-image is to listen to what people say about you. But
there is something even more valuable than what Burns suggests.
It is to be able to see yourself as God sees you. In fact, the only
really adequate self-image comes from an acceptance of the divine
evaluation of our lives.

Fortunately, God has not been at all reticent in this area and
has said plenty about His evaluation of people.

The ironic thing about God's evaluation of people is that He
appears to go right along with what the extremists say on both sides
of the self-image argument. Some passages of Scripture imply that
we should consider ourselves as worthless as the woman who failed
even at suicide. On the other hand, some Scripture statements
describe people as if the ultimate victory is theirs and absolutely
nothing can stop them. So what is the balanced view? Where is the
truth about self-image to be found?

Wandering Sheep

Perhaps the best known of all psalms, the 23rd, has some answers
to this problem. This psalm is the testimony of one who needed
and found a shepherd. Careful study reveals that the writer was
perfectly thrilled with the Shepherd he discovered and was
thoroughly enjoying his relationship with the Shepherd.

Presumably, therefore, the writer of Psalm 23 felt like a sheep
in many ways and in his capacity as a sheep was finding some real
answers in the Shepherd. This is the first clue to a healthy self-
image. The sheep image!

Perhaps you feel I have stretched things a little (or a lot) to
arrive at my conclusion, but I would remind you that the sheep
concept of man is quite compatible with other Scripture. "All we
like sheep have gone astray; we have turned every one to his own
way" (Isa. 53:6).

I have no expert knowledge of sheep but I have had considerable
unpleasant experimental knowledge of them. I was brought up in

a part of England known for its sheep rearing. In fact, they say that people don't die in those parts; they just turn into sheep! That, I doubt! But I do not doubt that it would be hard to find more stupid animals than sheep.

For some reason, sheep have a remarkable aptitude for getting lost. They can be perfectly at home in a pleasant pasture, until one revolutionary spirit among them finds a hole in the fence. In less time than it takes to tell they will desert the grass and head for the hole. In five minutes flat there won't be a sheep in the pasture and there will be hundreds on the road. Honking horns, bleating lambs, screeching tires, baaing ewes turn the quiet countryside into bedlam. All because some sheep decided to go astray, leading many others after it.

Now, any sensible sheep would survey such chaos and say, "Baaaaaaa—it was better in the pasture, let's go back again." Does that ever happen? No way. The sheep will mill around creating more and more chaos until a dog arrives. Then they will all head off in the opposite direction from the dog, regardless of where that will lead them!

There is something vaguely disturbing about sheep behavior especially as it relates to human behavior. People do have a great tendency to desert what is good for them, believing something better is just out of reach. To them "the grass is always greener" on the other side of the fence.

Herd instinct is just a polite expression for what turns out to be flock folly! We head after strong leaders with great enthusiasm, rarely stopping to check *where* they are leading us. There is an inbred propensity to go wrong in every human being, and failure to admit this must inevitably lead to an innacurate self-image.

Scripture is full of illustrations of this point. Many great figures of the faith had this in common: they recognized their own inbuilt bias to sin, their disturbing ability to go wrong. Some of them have their failures recorded in frightening detail: David, Saul, Moses, Peter, Paul, John Mark. And this is no accident. These things are recorded for our benefit, for unless we come to terms with our own failure, rebellion, and sin (the sheep syndrome), we will never have a realistic and accurate self-image.

"I Shall Not Want"

The other side of the coin is that any sheep who goes about things God's way can have a self-image that allows it to say things such as "I shall not lack anything" / "I will fear no evil" / "My cup runneth over." This is the language of an outgoing, almost exuberantly aggressive person. But this is exactly what the Lord talked about when He told His unsuspecting disciples, "Behold, I send you forth as sheep in the midst of wolves" (Matt. 10:16).

This appears at first to be totally contradictory. If I am to think of myself as a sheep, how can I think I will be strong enough to frighten wolves? On the other hand, if I can frighten wolves, why pretend I'm a sheep? Am I a sheep, or am I a wolf-frightener? Am I a helpless, hopeless failure, or am I invincible?

Rather than wrestle with this problem, many people decide to settle for one or the other. We do not have the privilege of deciding "either, or." The real picture is in both.

"The Lord Is My Shepherd"

Shepherdless sheep and sheep with shepherds are totally different. It's the shepherd who makes the difference. The Lord Jesus is the Good Shepherd, who not only gives His life for the sheep but also "knows them, calls them by name, and leads them" (see John 10).

When an adequate relationship exists between a sheep who freely admits his need of shepherding and the Shepherd who cares and leads in love and wisdom, the sheep begins to demonstrate great qualities not apparent previously. He never pretends to be anything more or less than a sheep, but he never settles for a life-style that is less than the result of most unusual input from the Shepherd.

The simple phrase, "The Lord is my Shepherd" says it all. Note carefully, the One of whom the sheep speaks: the LORD. We are familiar by now with all that this name implies. Never forget that this remarkable LORD has accepted responsibility to act as Shepherd to insignificant individuals. To believe this does more for the fractured self-image than anything else that I know.

The note of personal relationship is emphasized by the word *my*. It can't get any more intimate than that. Some people talk about God in generalities but are reluctant to get personal about Him. To say that Christ is real and relevant to them personally is more than they can manage. To profess intimacy with Him is to them the gravest embarrassment. But He looks for as personal a commitment from us as He offers to us.

The absolute certainty of the whole relationship is found in one tiny word right in the middle of the statement: *is.* No *ifs* or *buts,* just a clear *is.* Put it all together and you have the kind of conviction that makes sheep into wolf-chasers. Mice into men. The inadequate person into an adequate person.

Lying in Green Pastures

In all probability you have never had an uncontrollable urge to make a sheep lie down. Just in case this should happen to you, let me save you some trouble. Sheep are such anatomical oddities that the only way to their haunches is through their stomachs. In other words, you can't make a hungry sheep lie down. But if you can only fill its stomach it will find a quiet place, lie down, and contentedly ruminate on how good things are under the shepherd's control. Contentment is the word we must emphasize at this point, for contentment is a missing ingredient in our society. We live in a discontented age.

There is such frightening pressure on people to prove themselves. The demands of our society are such that, in order to be acceptable, many people are about to destroy themselves in the feverish acquisition of status symbols and the like. And when they are acquired, the preservation of these symbols appears to demand almost as much time and energy and to produce as many phobias and ulcers as the acquisition.

But what bliss to be content! To have no overwhelming desire to prove anything. To be able to look the world in the eye and say, "World, look at me, no more than a sheep who is content to be all and only what the Shepherd wants me to be. Take me or leave me, I'm nothing more than this. I have no desire to try to fulfill all society's expectations of me. I have little interest in piling up the things that society says are necessary for my well-being. I'm content."

Still Waters

Under stormy waves are quiet waters. Down where the fish live. A few years ago I went scuba diving in a fabulous coral reef. The small boat from which we were operating was tossed like a cork on the choppy sea but once we got under the surface the silence was deafening. Green light filtered through banks of multi-colored coral. Ridiculous shaped fish swam past us with utter disinterest, and in the weightlessness of the quiet deep we swam and relaxed.

Many of our storms are self made. In the mad crazy desire to be something that we are not or to compensate for what we'll never be, we get into all kinds of choppy waters. But there is an alternative; it is to allow the Shepherd to lead into the places of quiet and peace. Given the chance, He will.

This is not to suggest that *all* storms are self made. Innumerable situations for which we cannot be held responsible may hit us with the force of a southwesterly gale. Nevertheless, the principle is the same. Even in these storms there is a commitment on the part of the Lord to lead into peaceful waters—even while the storm continues to rage.

"He Restoreth My Soul"

I know what you're thinking. "All this peace and contentment business is all right but it just doesn't work out that way. In fact, that kind of talk only makes me feel more guilty that I'm not that way."

I'm glad you thought that, because I agree with you! Obviously, you are going to have moments when you feel that the roof has fallen in on your sheep pen and it will take all you have to survive. You reserve the right once in a while to come apart at the seams! And even if you don't admit it, you will anyway. The Lord allows for this and "restores your soul."

Some time ago a young man came to see me. He was doing a paper for his communications class at the university, and he had chosen to use my ministry as the basis of his project. He arrived in my study at the end of a day in which I had written a chapter of this book, prepared a sermon outline, done two TV shows, counseled two or three people, met with the missions committee, and I forget what else. Grinning he stretched out his hand and said, "How're you doing, Pastor?"

"Pooped," I replied. His smile froze.

When we had concluded our business, he said an interesting thing, "Thank you for letting me see that you get tired. I thought you didn't have that kind of problem." That was very gracious of him but he obviously hadn't been thinking too clearly. Of course, I get tired and discouraged, "weary, worn, and sad," but I don't have to stay that way. "He restores my soul."

"Paths of Righteousness"

Fear of making a wrong move paralyzes many people. I am constantly asked to counsel with those who really want me to make up their minds for them. They are so anxious to be right in their decisions and so unsure of their own ability to discern the way to go that they try to put the responsibility on other shoulders.

I firmly believe that counsel and advice should be readily shared among those who wish to do the right thing, but something important must be stressed at this point. "He leads me in the paths of righteousness for His name's sake." The Lord is concerned that His sheep go the right way for His sake. In fact, He is more concerned that His sheep go the right way than they can ever be. So He is prepared to make the way clear to the unsure and to direct those who will accept His direction.

This takes much of the stress out of living, because if the Lord has promised to lead in the path of His choice, the one thing the sheep has to do is maintain a right attitude of "followship" which will guarantee the blessing of His "leadership." There have been numerous occasions in my life when I have had no idea what I was getting into, but there was always quiet confidence that I was heading in the right direction. Not because I claim infallibility but because at the time in question I knew I was trusting the Lord to make the right path open to me.

It may sound as if this approach will destroy human insight and decisiveness. This is not the case, for the one who follows the Lord will need to exercise all these faculties and act in dependence as well. So check out your options, evaluate your decisions, get all the advice you can, explore the consequences, and then in dependence on the Shepherd to stop you if you're wrong, go ahead.

"The Valley of the Shadow"

Some people fear death. Others fear dying. Most fear both. Some fear neither, and the sheep is one of them. There is, of course, considerable trepidation in all our lives when we are faced with the unknown. And death is certainly unknown to all of us from an experimental point of view. So apprehension is perfectly understandable and permissible, but stark fear is not. The reason is plain to see: "Thou art with me" (v. 4).

The One who is with the Christian in death and dying is the One who has been there already and come through with flying colors: the Risen Lord. If it is true, therefore, that the "last enemy" is death, it is great news indeed to know that the One who has blown death wide open in resurrection is "with me."

I am not suggesting that the person who believes this should do anything to precipitate his own demise, either by his own hand or by lack of care. I do believe, however, that this kind of fearlessness is magnificent to behold in the person who is resting in the Lord. It may thrust him out to work in the trouble spots of the world with equanimity. It may lead him to work in areas that others shun. It will certainly equip him to meet the frightening situations of modern living with considerably more composure than the average person.

He has a firm conviction, you see, that the Lord of the valley will take him through the valley until He decides that it is time to go home. Then when the Lord decides it's time for him to go, the Christian can go with joy. Dead on time!

"Rod and Staff"

The shepherd's equipment was unsophisticated. Just rod and staff. But they were all that he needed. They were applied with two things in mind: protection and correction. When marauding animals came along, the shepherd would whack them with the rod. When the wandering sheep fell over a cliff, the staff would pull them back to safety. When they needed a poke, they would get it from rod or staff.

All this poking and prodding and whacking doesn't sound too appealing does it? To sheep it is. "Thy rod and Thy staff they comfort me!" It's a joy to know that you are protected and will be corrected. Protected from the dangers that will come upon you unawares. Corrected when you do things that will unnecessarily get you into trouble.

Some people can't stand to be corrected, and they are hard to live with. They impose their views and ideas with such vehemence that it is quite clear they are unsure of themselves and their arguments. But when people are open to the rebuke of the Lord, however administered, they become much more balanced and amenable.

"In the Presence of Mine Enemies"

I get the wildest picture in my mind when I read verse 5 of this psalm. The old sheep is seated at a sumptuous sheep feast. The table is laden with all that a sheep could ever wish to eat. All around are wolves, licking their chops, growling and yapping. The sheep, however, is quite unperturbed. "Don't bother me, can't you see I'm busy."

The ability to keep one's cool is a delightful trait that appears to be the gift of an ever-decreasing minority. In fact, we almost seem to think we have to blow our fuses to assert our masculinity. Or we have to yell and wave our fists to let people know how important we are. But imperturbability is a joy to practice and behold.

Next time you stand in line for a plane ticket on a Monday morning with all the salesmen with blow-wave hairdos and patent leather shoes, don't join them in hassling the little girl at the counter. Try telling your enemies (impatience, arrogance, selfishness) to go away because you're busy resting in the Lord who is bigger than a ticket counter and greater than an airline schedule. You could even try commending the little girl for doing an impossible job well!

"My Cup Runneth Over"

Sheep do get their heads torn and their wool ripped at times. But they don't have to display their injuries to everyone. Neither do they have to sulk in a corner licking their wounds. They can have the oil of anointing and healing poured in by the Lord in overflowing measure.

In the business world there are numerous occasions when heads get butted and wool gets torn. Butting usually leads to more butting until someone really gets hurt. Fragile egos are shattered, careers go to the wall, reputations are shredded. But it does not have to be that way.

Go to the One who dispenses the oil of anointing. He knows, cares, and understands perfectly. You think He doesn't know what head butting is all about? A few moments in the quiet place with Him can save limitless hours in the office with the boss or on the couch with the psychiatrist.

"Goodness and Mercy"

There are only two things that we have to learn in this life. How to live and how to die! I think the sheep of Psalm 23 has learned both. As for life, the clear testimony of the sheep is "all the days of my life" I will experience the goodness and mercy of God. And when death comes along, "I will dwell in the house of the Lord forever."

That about sums it up! In closing, let's just take a moment to see if our self-image is such that, freely admitting our sheepish capacity for going wrong and gladly acknowledging our dependence on the Lord to lead and provide, we look at life and death with such equanimity that we honestly feel we have nothing to prove except that in the Lord we do not lack anything at all.

Psalm 27:1-3, 14

The Lord is my Light and my Salvation; whom shall I fear? the Lord is the Strength of my life; of whom shall I be afraid?

When the wicked, even mine enemies and my foes, came upon me to eat up my flesh, they stumbled and fell.

Though an host should encamp against me, my heart shall not fear: though war should rise against me, in this will I be confident.

Wait on the Lord: be of good courage, and He shall strengthen thine heart: wait, I say, on the Lord.

7

When Fear Comes Calling and Won't Go Away

A sound in an empty house! You were alone, but you thought you heard something—*or someone*—downstairs. Icy fingers gripped your insides, your mind froze. Fear had immobilized you.

It was your turn to stand up and say something. The person ahead of you had done a superb job, and you knew you couldn't match his performance. Your knees turned to rubber. Fear had got hold of you.

The phone rang at 1 A.M. Your kids were at the first party you had allowed them to attend. *There's been an accident!* you thought and your hand just wouldn't reach out to that phone. Fear had paralyzed you.

You were alone in a roomful of people. Everybody was enjoying the event except you! Nobody knew you and you didn't know them. You would have liked to have been included, but you hesitated to break into a group conversation. You longed to be noticed, but you were not sure you could cope if you were. You were afraid of the whole situation and vowed to yourself, *Never again.*

Fear has many faces, and they are all ugly!

Boss or Bossed

The force of fear is so great in our lives that it can become a totally controlling influence. It is common knowledge that the majority of people in hospitals around the Western world are there, not because of physical illness, but because of illness of the mind, the psyche. And one of the main contributory factors to psychological disturbance and emotional sickness is fear.

David, the psalmist, had no training in psychology, but he had a lot of experience with fear! And he had a lot of faith! So his psalm has a wealth of sound principles and personal testimony even if it lacks psychological terminology.

Personally, I welcome this, for while I have the profoundest respect for those who have studied the intricacies of the human psyche and can deal with its involved imbalances, I believe that the Word of God has illustrations and principles that can bring untold blessings to the fearful and the anxious.

David's problem was that he had been run off his throne, a victim of conspiracy from within his own family.* He had gone into hiding and was in desperate straits. He had set up a government-in-exile at Mahanaim, across Jordan and had organized his loyalist forces to meet the expected onslaught from his son, Absalom.

Absalom, in the meantime, had gathered all the outstanding young men to his cause, had publicly disgraced his father, and was preparing a great army to finish off David. Humiliated, outgunned, and heavily outnumbered by his enemies, David knew fear. But he had some great things to say about how to handle it.

What Causes Fear?

People get frightened for different reasons. People have differing personalities, and some appear to be more susceptible to fear than others.

The Greek doctors of old had some interesting theories. They believed that personality was determined by the fluids that sloshed around in people's bodies. Fatuous as this may seem, we still carry some of their thinking into our day by using the terms they coined. So the phlegmatic (excess phlegm), the sanguine (excess blood), the choleric (excess bile), and the melancholic (excess black bile) are expressions with which we are familiar.

---

* Bible students are not agreed in identifying this psalm with a particular event in David's life. Many believe it relates to the time of Absalom's rebellion, and that is the assumption here.

Some of these personality types seem more or less prone to fear than others, and there is no doubt that sometimes we attribute our fear or lack of it to our temperaments. However, this can be a dangerous over-simplification, because everybody is afraid of something and sooner or later will show it. So temperament does play a part but *only in terms of the things that frighten us, not whether or not we are ever afraid.*

The bully who attacks an elderly woman may, in actual fact, be more fearful than she is. This he may discover when he feels the sharp edge of her tongue and gets the point of her umbrella!

Various traumatic events can take place in our lives and leave deep scars. Some people nearly drown in childhood and for the rest of their lives have a mortal dread of water. (Most small boys have this dread without nearly drowning!) The man who is bitten by a dog may act on the principle "once bitten, twice shy" for the rest of his days.

The determinists among us are convinced that we are what we are because of the environment in which we live. Everything is determined by circumstances outside our control. This is a gross exaggeration, but like most exaggerations it contains an element of truth.

The boy who was raised by a domineering dad who ridiculed him every time he opened his mouth may well grow up to have an overwhelming dread of having to express himself in public. The young person raised in wartime under constant bombing, may well show some evidence of trauma in later years.

Then there is another cause of fear that is often overlooked but which for the purposes of this study may be more important than the temperamental, psychological, and environmental causes we have just mentioned. This cause is spiritual. To put it quite bluntly, sin can be the cause of great fears.

Your Fears Are Showing

Uncertainty concerning the future is an overwhelming problem for countless people. That is no wonder when we consider the environment in which we live!

On a global scale, there is marked uncertainty. World peace is as fragile as a porcelain figurine, and ideological forces of frightening power are flexing their muscles.

On a personal level, wives wonder if they are next in line to be traded in for a new model, as many of their friends have been. Kids sit in their rooms alone with their stereos, worrying whether their parents will stay together. Men are uncertain of their jobs, senior citizens are fearful of being unable to afford the luxury of staying alive. Anxiety and indecision are often caused by the fear that comes from uncertainty concerning the future.

Culpability concerning the past is another great cause of fear. There is a skeleton in the closet of most families, and the sheer fear of having the skelton rattle its bones out in the open is enough to frighten many people out of their wits. This kind of fear is often demonstrated by worry, suspicion, and various withdrawal habits, coupled with depression.

It is not uncommon for marriages to fall apart because one of the parties has been hiding the facts of premarital misbehavior from the other and lives in fear of the truth coming out.

Businessmen who have evaded their taxes often have no chance to enjoy the money they "saved" because they spend all their time worrying if they are going to get caught.

However, perhaps the biggest problem for most people lies neither in the past nor the future, but right now. Uncertainty concerning the future or culpability concerning the past are exceeded by inadequacy concerning the present.

You have seen students break out in a rash before an examination. We are all familiar with businessmen who have been intolerable at home when trying to finalize a big deal. Brides on their wedding day have been known to faint! As have bridegrooms! The sheer fear of not being able to cope is one of the most debilitating things known to man.

The big question is, "Can people who are afraid find some answers to their problems?" The answer to that must, to a certain extent, be dependent on the specific causes of the fear. Those who have chronic problems in this area should no doubt seek professional help. But I am certain that many answers to fear are to be found in passages like the psalms.

"The Lord Is My Light"

The small town where I was born in the northwest corner of England was famous for its rich seam of iron ore. For years the iron had been mined, and there were many deserted mine shafts and tunnels around the town. In the fall these deserted areas were suddenly alive with people picking the blackberries that grew there in profusion.

When blackberry picking palled, the spirit of exploration took over. I have vivid recollections of following rusty railroad tracks through wild landscape entertaining all kinds of adventurous thoughts in my young mind. One day I strode manfully into a deserted tunnel and very quickly found myself in the dark. Striding manfully quickly changed to thinking childishly, and I was just about to panic until I saw the light at the end of the tunnel. The fear went, and I quickly regained my manly stride.

For many of us the future is similar to a long dark tunnel, and like all tunnels of that nature it is a little scary. However, there is light at the end of the tunnel. In fact, this light is so bright that it shines right into the tunnel. The light I refer to is the same One of whom David spoke: "The Lord is my Light."

The future can be divided into two parts. The future that lies ahead of us up to the grave and the future that stretches ahead after the grave. The Lord sheds great light on both. He is the One who alone can give "grace to help in time of need." This is the light He sheds before us for every day of our lives. He promises at every time of need to give us the ability to handle it. To believe this and to live in the good of it is to banish the darkness and to flood the future with lgiht.

The old adage says it better than anything else I know,

> *"I don't know what the future holds,*
> *But I know the One who holds my future."*

Countless illustrations of this come to mind, both from my personal experience and from my contacts with hundreds of people who have found this to be true.

Then there is the matter of death and what lies beyond. As we have already pointed out, fear relating to death and dying is extremely common. But remember what the Lord said, "I am the

Resurrection and the Life: he that believeth in Me, though he were dead, yet shall he live" (John 11:25). This means, of course, that the Lord Jesus gives to all who trust Him the assurance that they have eternal life when they have Him.

The response of the believing heart to this kind of assurance is one of great joy and confidence. The believer has so much light banishing the darkness of uncertainty, that he may get as belligerent as Paul and shout, "O death where is thy sting? O grave where is thy victory?" (1 Cor. 15:55) When a person comes to the realization that the Lord is the light of his life, fear of the future dissipates quickly.

The Lord Is . . . My Salvation

Guilt can play havoc with a person's life. When fear of disclosure is added to the guilt, the person concerned becomes extremely miserable. Unless some deep down answer to the guilt and fear is found, the wellbeing of the individual may be jeopardized.

But what are we to expect as far as deep down answers are concerned? All sin is against God, and unless it is viewed in this perspective, no adequate answer for guilt can be discovered.

I am aware, naturally, that many counselors would strongly disagree with this statement. I insist on it nevertheless, for this reason, When we begin to see that God has laid down standards of behavior for which we are answerable to Him, we can understand how desperately important our actions really are. (This ought to be an encouragement for most of us need some kind of reassurance at one time or another that we are important.) When we see that our actions, important as they are, have been out of order, according to God's judgment, we can see that we are in serious trouble in our relationships with Him.

There is, however, a glorious side to this whole situation. The God to whom we are responsible and against whom we have sinned is ready, willing, and able to forgive us. The depth of His forgiveness is so great that He is free to declare us "Not guilty" in the Highest Court of heaven. This forgiveness comes because Christ has paid the penalty of our sins, allowing God to be perfectly justified in granting us forgiveness.

If a person sees himself as a sinner before God, needing to be forgiven by God, and then hears that Christ has died for this very purpose, he can begin to get excited about being forgiven. The language he uses to express this excitement may be something like: "The Lord is my Light and my Salvation."

Understanding that the Lord is Saviour helps us to grasp the greatness of being forgiven. And that leads to freedom of expression about the past life. When God has forgiven a person, a great openness about being forgiven results.

I know a young woman who, when she was in school, worked in a women's fashions store. She was unable to resist the temptation of the beautiful clothes all round her and began to steal them. Eventually she became so fearful and ashamed that she confessed her sin to the Lord and sought His forgiveness.

She then told her employer and asked for an opportunity to repay him. The employer was so moved by her repentance and desire to do the right thing that he helped her greatly.

When she told this story in our church, she concluded in a way I will never forget. Throwing her arms in the air in a great gesture of freedom, she said, "Any of you can look in any part of my life and there will be nothing hid. All is confessed, all is forgiven. It's great to be free."

This is the freedom from fear that many people are seeking. It comes only from a sense of the saving, forgiving power of Christ in a life.

"The LORD Is the Strength of My Life"
The terrible sense of inadequacy that so many people live with makes them dread the day-by-day situations they must face. It is hard to imagine how some are able to face daily challenges that they know they cannot meet. Sometimes it is their own fault. Their egos will not allow them to admit their own limitations, so they are driven to live in realms where they don't belong, endeavoring to be people they will never be.

But this is not the case with all. Some are where they belong but don't feel they can do what is expected of them. New mothers, new husbands, new recruits, all have the same fears. Tired salesmen, injured athletes, fading beauties know the same gnawing uncertainties.

What should people do in such situations? First, find out what the Lord wants them to be and do. Then they should see if what they want differs from His plans for them. Having cleared this up in their own minds, they must decide which way they intend to go. If they decide to make a commitment to be what He wants them to be, they can be sure of one thing. He will equip them to do it.

A word of caution at this point may be necessary. The Lord does not promise to make fading beauties stop fading or hurting athletes stop hurting. He may be trying to tell the respective beauty or athlete, by their very experience, that He has something else in mind for them. But He does promise to show us what He has in mind. Then, when we go along with Him, He works on our behalf.

This makes people rejoice in the midst of their busy lives. As they battle with the everyday details of work and responsibility, they can say, "The Lord is the Strength of my life."

The joy of this kind of dependence banishes all fear because the load of responsibility is on the Lord to provide the strength. And He never fails.

"Whom Shall I Fear?"

Having made his confident statement known, the psalmist asks the resounding question, "Of whom shall I be afraid?" and follows right through with, "Whom shall I fear?" This becomes an extremely difficult question to answer in the light of his commitment to the LORD. In fact, it is impossible to think of anyone who could frighten him or any circumstances that could unnerve him, since the Lord is his Light, Strength, and Salvation. Grades

As if to drive the point home, David recounts the ways in which he has seen his enemies fall over themselves as they came up against him. He goes so far as to say that even if he finds himself surrounded and overwhelmingly outnumbered, "in this will I be confident" (v. 3).

There is much about spiritual living that raises the hackles of unbelievers. One of the most infuriating things to them is what they call "escapism." What I have just said about the Lord being the answer to many of our fears would fall into that category in their thinking.

Note, however, what David said: ". . . *in* this will I be confident." There isn't a thought of escape in his mind. He's right in where the action is hottest and he intends to stay there, but while he's there, he is going to be confident.

This is the position of the believer. He is not looking for something that will allow him to escape from reality. Drink and drugs do that. But he knows Someone who allows him to face reality, however frightening, live with it, and refuse to be overcome by it. 4/7/2000

Time and space do not permit a fuller study of the balance of the psalm, but note the last verse. "Wait on the Lord: be of good courage and He shall strengthen thine heart: wait, I say, on the Lord."

The one who has learned to master fear becomes an encourager of the fearful. He goes out of his way to recognize the symptoms of fear in his friends and shares his own experience of the Lord with them. This is great therapy as well as great Christian principle. To know some answers and not share them is to do less than the Lord expects, while to minister to others is one of the quickest and safest routes to wholeness.

Loved → Takes away fears

FRIGHT | Perfect LOVE
Casts out Fear

Dale ran criticism
FLEE

Psalm 32

Blessed is he whose transgression is forgiven, whose sin is covered. Blessed is the man unto whom the Lord imputeth not iniquity, and in whose spirit there is no guile.

When I kept silence, my bones waxed old through my roaring all the day long. For day and night Thy hand was heavy upon me: my moisture is turned into the drought of summer. Selah.

I acknowledged my sin unto Thee, and mine iniquity have I not hid. I said, I will confess my transgressions unto the Lord; and Thou forgavest the iniquity of my sin. Selah.

For this shall every one that is godly pray unto Thee in a time when Thou mayest be found: surely in the floods of great waters they shall not come nigh unto him. Thou art my hiding place; Thou shalt preserve me from Trouble; Thou shalt compass me about with songs of deliverance. Selah.

I will instruct thee and teach thee in the way which thou shalt go: I will guide thee with mine eye. Be ye not as the horse, or as the mule, which have no understanding: whose mouth must be held in with bit and bridle, lest they come near unto thee.

Many sorrows shall be to the wicked: but he that trusteth in the Lord, mercy shall compass him about. Be glad in the Lord and rejoice, ye righteous: and shout for joy, all ye that are upright in heart.

8

When You Need a Lot of Forgiveness

Like everybody else, David had his good days and his bad days. Sometimes he wrote psalms of somber quality and other times he put an exuberant poem to music and sang to his heart's delight.

Psalm 32 is a song of joy. It starts with "Blessed is he . . " and finishes with "Be glad in the Lord, and rejoice . . ."

It is not hard to find the reason for David's joy. He has done something he ought not to have done and having accepted full responsibility for his actions and repented fully of them, he knows he has been forgiven. There is nothing like forgiveness for making the heart sing and the soul rejoice!

Augustine, the brilliant theologian of long ago, loved this psalm. This comes as no surprise to those who are aware of his reprobate life and his conversion to Christ. He, like David, had discovered the greatness of God's forgiveness and lived his life in the enjoyment of it.

When a young woman demonstrated her love and gratitude to the Lord in a rather overt fashion, the Pharisee in whose home the event took place expressed some degree of disapproval. The Lord, however, said, "Her sins which are many are forgiven; for she loved much: but to whom little is forgiven the same loveth little" (Luke 7:47). It is quite clear that those who know what it is to be forgiven know what it is to love the Lord in an unashamed way. Forgiven much, they love much, and loving much, they show it in no uncertain terms. But in the church there are many people who, like the Pharisee, are desperately embarrassed by any demonstration of love. Apparently they would be much less inhibited in their love for the Lord if they were more overwhelmed with a sense of forgiveness.

Sin in Four Varieties

The man in the street and the man in the pew often disagree. But they are strangely in accord in one unexpected area. The man in the street thinks that sin is killing and cheating and running around. The man in the pew thinks the same thing, but quotes the Ten Commandments to prove it. He also knows that the Bible condemns such things as pride, jealousy, greed, and lack of faith. But he doesn't really think these things are as important as the "big bad sins." This error on the part of Christians is serious, because sins like pride and jealousy and greed are the roots from which other sins spring. We must realize that roots are at least of equal importance to fruits.

Because many people have failed to understand sin they have little idea of the immensity of God's forgiveness. They think that they never did anything very bad so God never had to forgive anything very big. Which means that they can't be expected to love very greatly.

All this is dangerous nonsense. What could be a greater sin than to deny God the right to be God? What could be more heinous than for puny people to usurp the authority of Almighty God? What can possibly be more objectionable to God than to have His creatures make the things He has given them more important than the One who gave them?

Yet, there is not a person on this earth who has not been guilty of these sins on a continuing basis. These sins desperately need to be forgiven. These attitudes need to be rejected, for they have produced multitudes of sins before God.

The psalmist carefully spells out the variety and enormity of our sins in order that we might fully appreciate the far-reaching implications of forgiveness. The psalm deals with "transgressions, sin, iniquity, and guile."

Transgressions

To transgress is to trespass. When I was young, my parents and my brother and I used to take country walks on Sunday afternoons. One day I read a sign: *Trespassers will be prosecuted.* "Dad," I said, "What does that mean?"

"It means that if you go where you shouldn't, you'll be propped up and shot," he replied with a grin.

I heard the words but didn't understand the grin. Later, however, I learned that such notices let people know that there are places where they are not free to go and that if they do they must bear the consequences. This is the meaning of "transgression."

God has outlined limits of human behavior and has made it quite clear that He expects human beings to operate within those limits for their own good and the well-being of society. But to a large extent the human race has found these limits intolerable and has decided to cross them at will.

Man may call this kind of behavior "the challenging of out-moded mores" or "the overthrow of repressive relics of the Victorian era." God has a shorter name for it; He calls it transgression. Every time you or I step over the God-given limits of human behavior, we transgress, and from that moment we are responsible for that sin. Try to figure out how many times you have stepped into the forbidden territory of jealousy or selfishness or independence. All need to be forgiven. Blessed is the man whose transgression is forgiven.

Sin

In liturgical services it is customary to say something to the effect that "we have done those things which we ought not to have done and left undone those things which we ought to have done." Doing what we ought not is "trespass or transgression." Not doing what we ought is "sin."

There are numerous ways of knowing what we ought to do. Conscience lets us know this quite regularly. The little voice inside whispers, "Go on, speak out about that gross miscarriage of justice." But the mind calculates, *If I do speak out, will it spoil my chances of promotion?* So silence reigns, as sin is committed.

Horrific stories have appeared in the press concerning girls being attacked in places where at least 25 people were within ear-shot. They heard but they didn't respond. *Don't get involved. Protect your own interests. You might get hurt.* So selfishness reigned, as sin was perpetrated.

God's commands to us are not always in the negative: Thou shalt not . . ." Many commands are negative, and they are the happy hunting grounds of "trespass." Many other commands are positive, "Thou shalt . . ." They are the areas in which sin flourishes. Sit down and think about this. Try to evaluate the regularity with which you have failed to do what you ought to have done. All that needs to be forgiven too.

Iniquity

Doing what we snouldn't and not doing what we should are the easiest areas of sinful behavior to understand. Now for something a little more complex. Iniquity is an inbuilt capability that perverts what is right and makes it into something wrong. It can sound great and yet be horrible. It can appear beautiful and yet be obnoxious.

For example, there are those who proclaim the gospel of peace in the political arena. They shout loud and long about the injustices of the political regimes under which people live. They promise great things in the name of freedom, but they don't always deliver. In fact, it is a sad thing to see what has been the lot of many who believed the evangelists of peace and freedom. They have found themselves in totalitarian regimes at best or Gulag Archipelagoes at worst.

What about the "gift to charity" that is proclaimed as a sacrifice but is really cheap advertising by way of a tax write-off? Or what do we say about the "prayer," offered in a small group, that is nothing more than a tirade directed at another person present, with all the right people listening?

Peace is right. Freedom is right. Prayer and giving are right, but iniquity can get a stranglehold on them and make them wrong. Every time that happens, sin is committed and our weight of responsibility increases.

Guile

Iniquity is the perverting of that which is right, but *guile* is the projecting of that which is false. Hypocrisy is a good word to describe it, particularly when we remember that the root meaning of hypocrisy is "play acting," or "performing behind a mask." Behind a mask is where much of our living takes place.

A good German friend of mine once ripped off my mask when I didn't even realize I was wearing one. He called me late at night and said, "Hello, how are you?"

I replied, "Fine! Hey, it's good to hear your voice."

With great German candor he replied, "Typical Englishman! Polite even when I wake you up at night. You are not pleased to hear my voice. You think I am stupid for calling at this hour. Why don't you say so?"

"All right, if you insist," I replied. "What on earth do you want at this hour of the night, you clown."

But he was right, I was behaving behind my mask.

Things get much more serious, of course, when matters of greater importance are involved. In fact, we can get so caught up in our own guile that we play games with God. We tell Him things we don't mean. We sing praise to Him that isn't true. We promise things we have no intention of performing. We become skilled at projecting that which is less than the truth.

Have you ever thought, *If only I had gotten into sin in a big way, I could have been forgiven in a big way and then I couldn't help but love God in a big way?* Will you promise never to think like that again? Because the truth of the matter is, you did get into sin in a big way. Day after miserable day, you transgressed and sinned and acted in iniquity and guile. You have constantly done what was forbidden, have left undone what was required, have perverted that which is right, and have projected that which is false. But what a thrill to know that it is the greatness of your sin which qualifies you for the vastness of forgiveness. And it is the knowledge of His forgiveness that leads to love and commitment.

The Psalms of Paul

When someone asked Martin Luther which were his favorite

psalms, he said, "The Pauline Psalms" (The Psalms of Paul). His quizzical point was that, while Paul didn't write any psalms that we know of, he did use David's quite freely. Psalm 32 is one of those Paul used (see Rom. 4:6-8). It is understandable that Luther enjoyed Paul's psalms so much, because Luther had some real problems finding peace with God and a sense of forgiveness. He tried to do all that he had been taught but still felt guilty. When he finally understood from the Scriptures that salvation, forgiveness, justification, and all the other blessings of God are made available to man on the basis of God's grace rather than man's efforts, he was almost beside himself with joy.

Paul was the great exponent of this doctrine of "justification by grace through faith," but he didn't invent it. David knew it. Abraham experienced it. In fact, down through the ages, men and women have come to God for the cleansing and forgiving they don't deserve but which God freely gives.

There are three aspects of forgiveness that David mentions in the psalm. He uses the terms *forgiven, covered,* and *not imputed.* Each has depths of meaning that we should understand.

The Meaning of Forgiveness

We are all familiar with the term "scapegoat." When a basketball team loses most of its games, something has to be done about it. The reason for the failure may well be that they don't have any good players, but, as they can't get rid of all the players, they have to find someone who can be held responsible. So they fire the coach. He becomes the scapegoat. The idea being that he is made responsible for the shortcomings of the whole outfit.

The original scapegoat was part of the Hebrew system of sacrifice and forgiveness. A goat would be selected by the high priest, who would lay his hands on its head, confess over it the sins, transgressions, and iniquities of the people, and thereby, in ceremonial fashion, put the weight of the sin on the goat. The animal was then sent away into the wilderness, and the children of Israel had a graphic reminder of how God puts our sins away from Him. This is the basic meaning behind the word *forgiven* that David uses.

Since Christ came, the scapegoat is no longer necessary for He bore our sins. He was separated from the Father because of our sins. He died and rose again, burying our sins "in the depths of the sea," removing them "as far as the east is from the west" so that God can now say to us, "Your sins and iniquities I will remember no more."

Many times as I have prayed with people who longed for forgiveness, they have testified to the inexpressible sense of relief that flooded their souls when they knew that their sins had been taken away.

Out of Sight

"Blessed is he . . . whose sin is covered" (v. 1). God is committed to forgiving sin so thoroughly that He will put it out of His mind, out of remembrance, and out of sight. This is a great truth to grasp.

Often I have found myself in a position where I have been required to forgive someone, but the thoughts that I harbor concerning that person reveal that my forgiving has certainly not included forgetting. But real forgiveness forgets.

During the last few days, as I write this, I have had to deal with a marital situation that was extremely serious because of the unfaithfulness of the wife. I believe there has been real confession and forgiveness, but the husband is going to have a struggle forgetting what has taken place. Eventually I am sure that he will, but for the present there will have to be a period of healing and reassuring. I think we can all understand this. But what a joy it is to know that God covers up our sins so effectively that they will never be thought of or discussed again.

My wife, Jill, told me that she was worried at one time about something she had done. As she was praying, she said, "Lord, You remember that awful thing I did . . ." She sensed that He replied, "No, I don't remember. Jill, if *you* want to remember what I forgot, that's your privilege. But I would suggest you learn to forget what I have forgotten."

We don't talk much about "imputing" these days (v. 2). We use the word "reckoning." When the Bible says that God will not reckon our sins to us, it means that He will not put them on our account. Obviously, all debts have to be charged to some account, and the great news of forgiveness is that God places our debts on Christ's account. He accepts full responsibility for them.

The terrible debts that we could never repay have been transferred from our account, so we now have the possibility of living lives that will accumulate some real assets to the glory of God. When we begin to understand the greatness of our sin and the depth of God's forgiveness, the foundation is laid for a whole new experience of life.

The Heavy Hand

The experience of finding forgiveness is not without its pressures. The psalmist explains something of the battle that went on in his life as he became increasingly conscious of his sin, and more aware of the necessity for dealing with it. David was under considerable pressure from the Lord, which he describes in such graphic phrases as, "my bones waxed old through my roaring" / "Thy hand was heavy upon me" / "my moisture is turned into the drought of summer" (vv. 3-4).

In other words, David was suffering from such guilt and conviction that he was dry and depressed and thoroughly upset. The longer he "kept silence," the worse it became, but when he came to the point of "acknowledging and confessing," he was able to say, "Thou forgavest my sin" (v. 5.).

Bits and Bridles

Beware of the mistaken idea that once confession has been made and forgiveness received, we are free to go on as before. Be perfectly clear in your mind that being forgiven does not leave you free to go on in the same way. Rather, it introduces you to a new responsibility to be different. When the Lord forgave the woman who had committed adultery, He didn't say, "OK, forget it." He insisted that having been forgiven she should, "Go, and sin no more" (John 8:11).

Don't be like an unthinking horse that has to be held by bit and bridle to keep him under control (v. 9), but open yourself up to the instructions of the Lord and act in obedience to Him. Then He promises to guide. And He will not lead us into temptation, but will deliver us from evil. The ongoing of the forgiven life is dependence on the Lord to instruct and a response to the Lord in obedience. The Lord then undertakes to lead in the right path.

Mercy Shall Compass Him

To be surrounded by hostility makes people edgy and suspicious. What happens, then, to people who are compassed by mercy? (v. 10) They begin to respond in more merciful ways to others. The forgiven are great forgivers. It is their desire to forgive.

Some years ago a fashionably dressed woman came to my study, very distressed. She had made a commitment to the Lord a few days earlier but had asked to see me because something was troubling her. She poured out an unpleasant story concerning an affair she had been having with one of her husband's friends. Then she insisted that her husband should know, and that I should tell him! That was a new experience for me!

After some discussion with the woman, I called the husband. When he arrived at my study, I told him what had happened. His response was a remarkable and beautiful thing to behold. Turning to his tearful and fearful wife he said, "I love you. I forgive you. Let's make a new start."

Many things had to be straightened out, and much hurt had to be healed, but his response of forgiveness, made possible by his own understanding of the forgiveness of God, became the basis of a new joy and a new life.

Bitterness and harshness do not belong in the forgiven heart. Love and joy and forgiveness flourish there. In your experience of the forgiveness of God, learn to forgive the boss who abused your willing spirit, the church that failed to meet your expectations, the spouse who hurt you, and the kids who disgraced you. God forgave you, didn't He?

Psalm 37:1-36

Fret not thyself because of evildoers, neither be thou envious against the workers of iniquity. For they shall soon be cut down like the grass, and wither as the green herb.

Trust in the Lord, and do good; so shalt thou dwell in the land, and verily thou shalt be fed. Delight thyself also in the Lord; and He shall give thee the desires of thine heart. Commit thy way unto the Lord; trust also in Him; and He shall bring it to pass. And He shall bring forth thy righteousness as the light, and thy judgment as the noonday.

Rest in the Lord, and wait patiently for Him: fret not thyself because of him who prospereth in his way, because of the man who bringeth wicked devices to pass. Cease from anger, and forsake wrath: fret not thyself in any wise to do evil. For evildoers shall be cut off: but those that wait upon the Lord, they shall inherit the earth. For yet a little while, and the wicked shall not be: yea, thou shalt diligently consider his place, and it shall not be. But the meek shall inherit the earth; and shall delight themselves in the abundance of peace.

The wicked plotteth against the just, and gnasheth upon him with his teeth. The Lord shall laugh at him: for he seeth that his day is coming.

The wicked have drawn out the sword, and have bent their bow, to cast down the poor and needy, and to slay such as be of upright conversation. Their sword shall enter into their own heart, and their bows shall be broken.

A little that a righteous man hath is better than the riches of many wicked. For the arms of the wicked shall be broken: but the Lord upholdeth the righteous.

The Lord knoweth the days of the upright: and their inheritance shall be for ever. They shall not be ashamed in the evil time: and in the days of famine they shall be satisfied. But the wicked shall perish, and the enemies of the Lord shall be as the fat of lambs: they shall consume; into smoke shall they consume away.

The wicked borroweth, and payeth not again: but the righteous showeth mercy, and giveth. For such as be blessed of him shall inherit the earth; and they that be cursed of him shall be cut off.

The steps of a good man are ordered by the Lord: and he delighteth in his way. Though he fall, he shall not be utterly cast down: for the Lord upholdeth him with his hand. I have been, young, and now am old; yet have I not seen the righteous forsaken, nor his seed begging bread. He is ever merciful, and lendeth; and his seed is blessed.

Depart from evil, and do good; and dwell for evermore. For the Lord loveth judgment, and forsaketh not His saints; they are preserved for ever: but the seed of the wicked shall be cut off. The righteous shall inherit the land, and dwell therein for ever.

The mouth of the righteous speaketh wisdom, and his tongue talketh of judgment. The law of his God is in his heart; none of his steps shall slide.

The wicked watcheth the righteous, and seeketh to slay him. The Lord will not leave him in his hand, nor condemn him when he is judged.

Wait on the Lord, and keep His way, and He shall exalt thee to inherit the land: when the wicked are cut off, thou shalt see it. I have seen the wicked in great power, and spreading himself like a green bay tree. Yet he passed away, and, lo, he was not: yea, I sought him, but he could not be found.

9

When Being Good Doesn't Seem to Pay

Few things are more infuriating than seeing rogues go free while honest men suffer. There is nothing more disturbing than knowing that the hard hit will get hit harder while the protected will get more protection. This is particularly true if you are trying to do the right thing and it goes sour on you while people around you are not even trying to do right and life is sweet for them.

The unfairness and injustice of life is one of the hardest things to take! We may even get so envious of the people who go their merry way of irresponsibility and illegitimacy that we feel our struggle for righteousness and justice is futile.

Others seem to get away with murder, and you can't get away with anything. You try to do an honest day's work. You endeavor to be honest and frugal, but the more you try to do things right the more you find you are not appreciated. You may even be ridiculed, while the other people get all the gravy.

When you look at some of the people in high places, you know they got there by shady means and stay there by even shadier tactics, and nothing can be done about it.

You know your boss is "adjusting" his tax returns, but he gets away with it. He has a plush office and a plusher secretary while your office is so small you have to go outside to turn a page. And you answer your own phone.

You know a kid who got busted for drugs when he was innocent.

He was framed by an unscrupulous cop. The kid is inside and the cop is free. It's all very maddening.

Green Bay Trees

Now if this sounds very unspiritual, tell David because these were the kinds of thoughts that passed through his mind. Such thoughts *should* be in the mind of the spiritual person because he is the one who ought to be carefully observing his society. It is he who should recognize the injustices in the world caused by the refusal of men to adhere to God's principles. He is the one who must not close his eyes to these things. He should be inquiring and searching and dealing with these issues.

David put it bluntly, "I have seen the wicked in great power, and spreading himself like a green bay tree" (v. 35). He also said that he had been fully acquainted with "evildoers" (v. 1), "workers of iniquity" (v. 1), and "the man who bringeth wicked devices to pass" and "who prospered in his way" (v. 7).

Tough But Necessary

People who try to do things God's way have a difficult road ahead of them. They are called to a life of conflict. Given a choice between a life of comfort and a life of conflict, most people naturally choose the former. But the one who is committed to Christ has, in making that commitment, chosen the latter. To go "His way" means exactly going His way, and He went the way of the cross.

Christ suffered not only the agony of Calvary but the anguish of rejection and the pain of misrepresentation. He knew what David meant when he talked of the wicked working "to slay such as be of upright conversation" (v. 14). This adds further pressure to the believer because, having chosen to follow Christ in the path of conflict, he finds that he is being attacked by those who are committed to nothing.

Turning the other cheek gets wearisome. Giving rather than receiving becomes expensive. Especially when you have the obligation to give but the receiver feels no responsibility to return anything. "The wicked borroweth and payeth not again; but the righteous showeth mercy, and giveth" (v. 21).

Having your good works abused, your sincere desire to help ridiculed, your sacrificial living mocked, and your responsible lifestyle turned to the advantage of the unscrupulous is hard to take. But such conflict and sacrifice and discipline are the ingredients that, mixed with faith, make a vital spiritual experience.

Wise Heads Prevail

Hot heads lose control, cool heads prevail. Inexperience overreacts, experience calculates more carefully. David wrote this psalm from the vantage point of old age. He had come a long way from the sheepfold. It was no fresh-faced shepherd boy talking here, but one who could say, "I have been young and now am old" (v. 25).

Years of hard experience had mellowed David into a man of deep insight, integrity, and balance. Innumerable experiences of failure and success, disappointment and delight had left their mark on him. But his conviction concerning his Lord, his faith in Him, and his absolute assurance that He would ultimately reign in righteousness had never wavered. David proclaimed this loud and clear.

God Will Ultimately Triumph

Living in a world of injustice and exploitation can be wearing on an individual. Feeling that everything is hopeless and useless, he may want to give up. But taking this course is not acceptable because it discounts the Lord. Through all our turmoil and disaster shines the fact that the Lord has gone on record that He will ultimately triumph. We have seen this repeatedly in the psalms, but specific phrases illustrate it in Psalm 37. "The Lord upholdeth the righteous" (v. 17); "the Lord knoweth the days of the upright" (v. 18); "and the enemies of the Lord shall . . . consume away" (v. 20).

Through all the difficulties of spiritual experience, the Lord will bring His people to an inheritance which "shall be for ever" (v. 18). This is a blow to all the forces that oppose the saints, for these forces can't win. They can frustrate and infuriate and intimidate, but they can't obliterate because the Lord has reserved the final triumph for Himself. All the agencies of oppression that have unjustly worked in disregard of God's principles will finally be thwarted. One day they will have to watch those they despised and oppressed rejoicing in the glory.

Those same hostile forces and agencies will also feel the triumph of God in their own experience. "The wicked shall perish" (v. 20). The Lord has stated categorically that everyone who practices injustice, who specializes in oppression, who scorns divine principle had better beware: "His day is coming" (v. 13).

Good Will Eventually Prevail

It is a short step from the triumph of God to the prevailing of good. God and good are closely related. Read verses 9 through 15 carefully and examine all the statements concerning the eventual destruction of wickedness and the wicked one. Then in total contrast, check the statements regarding those who have followed the Lord.

The wicked are going to see their plans backfire, their riches dissipate, their empires crumble. It is not too difficult to understand this even from modern history. The wicked prosper, the unscrupulous strut around, the rogues laugh, and the rascals grin and wink—but *where are their predecessors?*

It is not necessary to name names, but those who used to hold power unjustly have fallen and departed. They have gone to their reward, and the gains of their abuses have gone into other pockets. Empires built on injustice have fallen! Power structures based on greed have left the greedy both empty handed and empty hearted. This is how it has always been, and this is how it is going to be till the end of time.

Down But Not Out!

Meanwhile, the ones who endeavor to resist the pressures and swim against the tide will finally discover that they chose the right course. In words reminiscent of the Sermon on the Mount, David said, "The meek shall inherit the earth; and shall delight themselves in the abundance of peace" (v. 11).

With this in mind, the "good man" steps out knowing that his steps are "ordered by the Lord" (v. 23). Of course, some of those steps are steep, and many a well-meaning believer has tripped over the most trifling problem, but even when this happens, he has the assurance that "though he fall, he shall not be utterly cast down" (v. 24). Down he may be, but not out!

It is of the utmost importance that these principles be understood. When they are grasped and believed, there is the real possibility that people may learn to cope with injustice and abuse. More, they may demonstrate to a watching world the reserves of strength and resources for living that many of those watching do not possess. In this way, they will have a testimony to the world that is sadly needed at this time.

The Early Church clearly showed to an incredulous world that Christians could take unbelievable abuse, suffer incredible hardship, and triumph so thoroughly that even her oppressors and abusers were compelled to come to Christ.

The same has been the case in many churches under totalitarian regimes and in areas of the world where suffering has become a fact of life for multitudes of people.

Trust and Do

This psalm contains very specific instructions for those who endure injustice and who understand that God will finally triumph and good ultimately prevail. I am glad for these instructions because simply believing that "it will all come out in the wash" and "there'll be a brighter day tomorrow" leaves something to be desired in terms of knowing exactly how to cope now.

"Trust in the Lord, and do good" (v. 3) is easy enough to understand if not always easy to do. This heart attitude of trust in the Lord, who will ultimately triumph and who is committed to rewarding right and punishing wrong, is vital. If I can trust God to work out the final results, I need not worry about them myself. This leaves me free to get on with doing the right thing, knowing that God will look after the guy who is doing the wrong thing. My natural tendency is to do just the opposite. I feel inclined to get after the guy who did the wrong thing and make him pay for it while ignoring the thing that God has told me to do.

Apply this to a marital situation for example. A husband does something wrong and harms the relationship. The wife finds out and devotes her considerable talents thereafter to making him pay for it. She denies him his conjugal rights and generally concentrates on "getting even." This doesn't help anything but makes matters a thousand times worse. No doubt she had a raw deal. No one disputes that, but there is equally no doubt that she reacted to injustice the wrong way. She should have said to herself and her husband, "What you did was wrong, and you're answerable to God, so I'll let Him deal with you. Since I'm answerable to Him too, I'm going to concentrate on doing the right thing by you." That is trusting God to do His part and obeying God in doing your part. Trusting and doing.

Delight and Desire

An unfortunate thing about injustice is that it makes you concentrate on it. When something goes wrong for you, it is sometimes difficult to remember all the things that have gone right. And it is even more difficult to remember the Lord in it all. But "delight . . . in the Lord" is what David insisted we should do (v. 4).

To delight in the Lord while suffering injustice requires great discipline of mind and will. But there is a beautiful incentive. "Delight thyself also in the Lord, and He shall give thee the desires of thine heart" (v. 4). This promise needs a little explanation because it can be misunderstood. It does not mean that you can ask for and anticipate receiving anything your selfish heart may desire. It means that if the Lord is your delight, He will give you desires that are new and beautiful. Your desires will originate with the Lord.

Think about the possibilities! If the wife we described were to delight in the Lord instead of riveting her attention on her raw deal, she would get a whole new set of desires from Him. She would desire to work out a reconciliation instead of concentrating on recrimination. She would desire to show grace more than grief, and love more than hate. And that would certainly be to everyone's advantage.

Commit and Trust

Once injustice has been experienced, reaction sets in immediately. If this is not dealt with quickly, the shoulder may develop a chip.

Chips soon become personal crusades, and in no time at all injustice will be added to injustice.

There is another approach to the problem. The Lord Jesus used it to great effect. "When He was reviled, [He] reviled not again . . . but committed Himself to Him that judgeth righteously" (1 Peter 2:23). This approach did not allow Christ to escape the cross, but it did allow Him to glorify the Father in the way He handled personal injustice. And how did He handle it? By committing Himself to the righteous Judge.

This is exactly what the psalmist insists we should do, but notice that in addition to "Commit thy way unto the Lord," it adds, "trust also in Him" (Ps. 37:5).

Some years ago I was preaching in a town in the Deep South. A woman had accepted responsibility for getting me to the church on time. She was very large and had a large car which she filled with a large number of friends. I was required to squeeze into the back seat in less space than it takes. We took off down the road at a terrifying pace and shot straight through a stop sign. Quite frankly, I was frightened out of my evangelical mind.

The main problem was the lady insisted on talking face to face with me at the same time she was driving. Since I was huddled in the back seat, you understand that this meant that she couldn't concentrate on me and the road. She chose me.

By stepping into her car, I had committed myself to her driving, but I can assure you that after the first 100 yards I didn't trust her at all. Not infrequently you will find that commitment made to Jesus Christ may similarly wear thin when unwanted things happen. But David exhorts us to "trust also in Him." And the result of this trusting and committing will be: "He shall bring to pass" (v. 5).

It is just as if the Lord is saying, "Don't try to deal with the injustices of life yourself. Trust Me and I will handle your case."

Rest and Wait

No doubt some of you are ready to retort, "That's OK, but how do you expect me to sit back and take all this abuse without any kind of reaction?" I agree that would not be a natural response, but that is what makes it so interesting. It is a spiritual response. Instead of handling the thing yourself, you learn to trust God to work on your behalf. Far from being totally committed to redressing your own injustices, you are content to believe that God will ultimately work things out.

The very idea of "ultimate" adds a dimension that is so often missing. We tend to want immediate answers to our problems and immediate redress of our ills. But God does not work at our frantic pace. He sees things in the light of eternity rather than in the glare of time.

God is thinking of perfecting people for glory rather than protecting people from unpleasantness. In fact, He may use the injustice and the unpleasantness as a lesson to lead us further in our relationship with Him. The Apostle Paul certainly learned things in prison that he would never have learned elsewhere. I'm sure that he often thought his treatment was unjust. Nevertheless he learned to be patient and faithful in his smelly cell. Like David, his attitude was to "rest in the Lord and wait patiently for Him" (v. 7).

Three Don'ts

After such an impressive list of things to do, there are three things not to do. First, don't fret about it. Fret means literally to burn or consume, so we can say don't get hot under the collar about what is happening to you. Don't let it eat you up. Don't get so consumed with it that you can't think of anything else.

Second, "Cease from anger" (v. 8). Don't get mad about it. Plenty of people in plenty of places are getting plenty mad about what has happened to them. And I can understand their being upset, but the Lord has told us that it is not necessary or helpful for us to get angry about it, if we really trust Him in our lives.

Third, "Depart from evil" (v. 27). Don't play with the wicked at their own game. One bad turn does not deserve another. Evil reactions to evil deeds are still evil. So don't stoop to sin in response to sin. Injustice is no cure for injustice.

What About Social Injustice?

When the Scripture speaks against reacting to personal injustice, it is not referring to the reactions we should have to the social injustices being dished out to others. It is my firm conviction that those who love the Lord and respect His ways should be constantly on the alert for abuses of His principles in society and should also be ready to act on behalf of the oppressed in the name of the Lord. But in all their activities they should never stoop to evil. We cannot do evil that good may come of it.

Psalm 42

As the hart panteth after the water brooks, so panteth my soul after Thee, O God. My soul thirsteth for God, for the living God: when shall I come and appear before God?

My tears have been my meat day and night, while they continually say unto me, "Where is thy God?" When I remember these things, I pour out my soul in me: for I had gone with the multitude, I went with them to the house of God, with the voice of joy and praise, with a multitude that kept holyday.

Why art thou cast down, O my soul? and why art thou disquieted in me? hope thou in God: for I shall yet praise Him for the help of His countenance.

O my God, my soul is cast down within me: therefore will I remember Thee from the land of Jordan, and of the Hermonites, from the hill Mizar. Deep calleth unto deep at the noise of Thy waterspouts: all Thy waves and Thy billows are gone over me.

Yet the LORD will command His lovingkindness in the daytime, and in the night His song shall be with me, and my prayer unto the God of my life.

I will say unto God my rock, "Why hast Thou forgotten me? why go I mourning because of the oppression of the enemy?"

As with a sword in my bones, mine enemies reproach me; while they say daily unto me, "Where is thy God?"

Why art thou cast down, O my soul? and why art thou disquieted within me? hope thou in God: for I shall yet praise Him, who is the health of my countenance, and my God.

10

When Depression Blankets You Like a Cloud

"Buzz" Aldrin went to the moon. He returned to earth and found that he couldn't cope with the life to which he returned. First he went into serious depression and then he went into print and on to the talk shows to share his experience.

Winston Churchill, one of the "greats" of human history suffered terribly from depression. He said it followed him like "a black dog."

Ernest Hemingway, the rugged all male he-man author of best sellers like *For Whom the Bell Tolls* and *The Old Man and the Sea,* had such a problem in this area that he eventually took his own life.

Abraham Lincoln, whose "House Divided Against Itself" speech helped to win him the presidency, knew awful divisive doubt and depression in his own life.

Charles Haddon Spurgeon, one of the greatest preachers of all time, who was known for his sparkling wit and quick humor, nevertheless had a lifetime battle with depression which was caused by gout, the disease which led to his death at the age of 58.

Depression is all too common in today's world. The offices of doctors and psychiatrists, pastors and counselors are full to over-flowing with people suffering from this condition.

Most of us are all too familiar with the despondent look of those who are depressed. Everywhere we see the morose faces of people who are sinking under their circumstances. Tears and sighs, tales of woe and stories of broken hearts abound.

113

Many depressed people live alone. Their main source of company is the television, which makes them even more depressed. Soap operas churn out hours of interminable coffee cup discourses almost exclusively devoted to the nonsolving of problems. The news brings the depressing truth of our contemporary world right into their laps. Dramatic presentations seem to have a chilling infatuation with the more depressing aspects of our society. About the only relief available comes from the comedy programs, and they don't solve anything. They just help people escape reality for a half hour or so.

Depression is a major ill that affects more people than we imagine and infects them more than we realize.

What Causes Depression?

No doubt some people are more prone to depression than others because of their temperaments. If they tend to be introspective there is more chance of their getting depressed than if they are extroverts.

But it must be said that while introverts are more prone to depression than others, they are also usually more sensitive and concerned than others. So being an introvert is not all bad! Dr. Martyn Lloyd-Jones in his book *Spiritual Depression* writes, "Indeed I could make out a good case for saying that quite often the people who stand out most gloriously in the history of the church are people of the very type we are now considering. Some of the greatest saints belong to the introverts."

Physically disability can also lead to depression. In Spurgeon's case this was certainly true. Gout is an extremely painful illness centering in the big toe, of all places! (I'm sure even Spurgeon's humor had a hard time seeing the funny side of that at times!) But you don't have to suffer from gout to be depressed. Being overtired, or under undue stress for a sustained period, or having a prolonged illness will probably do the trick.

Spiritual Depression

I do not want to fall into the error of separating spiritual depression from depression caused by temperament or physical disability.

People are spirit, soul, and body, and all three are bound up together. But some people are depressed primarily because they have some real problems of the spirit. Sin can get one terribly down. Guilt can become so pervasive as to immobilize a person. And we must not forget to mention the considerable power of Satan as he can work in people's lives and lead them into the trough of depression.

One day as I was packing to go on a preaching trip to the Orient, I got an urgent call to a home. Arriving there I found the man of the house sitting looking at a point on the wall. His wife said he had been in that position for hours.

I told him, "You need to see a doctor because you may have a physical problem. He may recommend a psychologist if he thinks you have an emotional problem, but if you have a spiritual problem I may be able to help."

As soon as I said "spiritual" he showed the first sign of interest. So I explained forgiveness, justification, hope, heaven, eternal life, and all kinds of things that the Lord offers in the bundle of salvation. Suddenly he said, "I want to be forgiven." At that point I got cold feet. What if he had a tumor? I would be making matters worse. I felt strangely over my head but asking the Lord for wisdom, I took a deep breath and led the man in prayer.

When I returned from my tour, he met me in church with a great grin on his face. No more depression or morose feelings had come his way. He said, "I'm free of all that, and I know that I'm forgiven and have eternal life." I still made him see a physician!

David's Depression

The great men of the Bible were not immune to depression. John the Baptist understandably got depressed when he lay in his cell wondering what the Messiah was doing. Jeremiah wept copiously over the destruction of Jerusalem and because his own circumstances went from bad to worse. Job scratched himself with a broken piece of pottery and listened to his depressing friends give their advice. Elijah fell into a dark hole of depression after his victory on Mount Carmel.

But David's experience of depression as recorded in Psalm 42 is particularly helpful because he had much to say about how it felt and what he did about it. I often recommend a careful reading of this psalm to those who are having troubles with depression.

The circumstances of David's life were such that he had been deprived of many things he held dear. Not least was his regular attendance at a place of worship. It may seem to us that he was too dependent on the place and that he should have been able to worship the Lord anywhere. In all fairness, though, we have to admit that places and people play a big part in our experience of the Lord. So great was David's disappointment that he felt he had lost the sense of the Lord's presence. There was a tinge of desperation in his voice when he said, "As the hart panteth after the water brooks, so panteth my soul after Thee, O God."

Self Pity

People hadn't helped much either. Some of them had taken the opportunity to kick him while he was down. Continually, they had been sneering at him, "Where is your God?" This only served to upset David more. It's bad enough being out of touch with the Lord but it is 10 times worse when people notice it and start to deride you because of it. His tears had flowed, but I want you to note that he said, "My tears have been my meat day and night" (v. 3). He had fallen into the state of being so sorry for himself that he was feeding on his unfortunate situation. This led him deeper into depression. There was no relief. Day and night he cried. Hour after hour he succumbed to his feelings. There appeared to be no way out of his predicament.

His mind was fixed on his sorrows: "When I remember these things" (v. 4). Over and over he dwelt on the dismal disappointments of his life until he could think of nothing else. He shared these things with nobody. Brooding alone he said, "I pour out my soul in me" (v. 4). Living in the fading memories of the "good old days" he recounted how he "went with them to the house of God, with the voice of joy and praise" (v. 4).

The details of David's circumstances may differ from ours, but the experience of his depression is not at all removed from the symptoms suffered by so many. Self pity, brooding, withdrawal, morose reminiscing, introspection have been the painful lot of the depressed in all ages.

Admit the Truth

Fortunately David did not only recount his depression. He went into some detail as to how he coped with his feelings. The first thing to note is that he was realistic enough to admit that he was depressed. "Why art thou cast down, O my soul?" he asked repeatedly (vv. 5, 11; 43:5). So there was no evasion on his part. He was depressed and he knew it and was prepared to admit it.

Not everyone who is depressed is prepared to be realistic in this way. It is sometimes easier to dwell on the unfortunate circumstances in which you find yourself than to admit that you are in bad shape. It's your condition, not your circumstances, that is really important.

If someone gets shot in the leg, there are two courses he could follow. He could sit down and ponder the fact that he got shot, take photographs of his wound, study books on ballistics and take a course in the psychological aberrations of potential assassins. Or he could say, "I'm shot. Get me to the doctor!"

If you've never done it before, do it now. Say aloud, "I am depressed!"

Bring the Lord into the Depression

Having admitted the truth of the matter, David then took another vital step. He related his depression to the Lord. It is no accident that the Lord is mentioned or referred to at least once in every verse of the psalm. Not always in the correct vein. But at least He was mentioned!

"Why hast Thou forgotten me?" is a very honest question. David felt that the Lord had overlooked his plight. And it is easy to feel that way. You don't need too many awkward situations before you are tempted to question God's relevance, faithfulness, or even His existence.

A little elementary Bible knowledge at this point goes a long way. "I will never leave thee nor forsake thee" (Heb. 13:5) and, "Lo, I am with you alway" (Matt. 28:20) are straightforward promises from the God who cannot lie. Provided we keep what we believe in front of how we feel, we can cope with temptations to doubt God. But if we allow how we feel to alter what we believe, we are in deep trouble.

A man may wake up feeling not very married. He goes to work and sees a cute little girl in the office and in no time at all he behaves as if he is not married. This would never have happened if he had kept the fact of his marital commitment in the forefront of his mind instead of allowing his feelings about his marriage to dominate. So it is with our relationship to the Lord.

Try a Little Detective Work

Once you have been honest about your condition and been consistent about the fact that you are the Lord's, it is time for a little detective work. Start delving into the situation in which you find yourself. Ask some pertinent questions. You may need help at this point because you can't think of any questions. Find a trusted friend who will level with you if you can't do it on your own. Then start asking yourself, "Why art thou cast down, O my soul?" Why, why, why?

But be very careful. David is not getting further into his self-pity asking, "Why did this have to happen to me?" or, "Why can't someone else have some bad luck instead of it always being me?" His question is factual and pertinent. "Why are you depressed, soul?"

This question, if handled honestly, may lead the depressed person into some deep personal discoveries. For instance, he may discover that his depression is the result of resentment. Because things have gone the way they have and the person concerned is angry with God and everyone else, he has sunk lower and lower into his own resentful mire.

Or he may discover that subconsciously he felt that he had a divine right of immunity from all problems. He may never have come to the elementary understanding of life that allows any sensible person to see that problems are inevitable in a sin-distorted world. And there, he should not be naive enough to think that he alone should go through life smelling roses.

Depressed people make discoveries like this only when they are wise enough to investigate into their own lives. Then they have to adjust to the answers they find to the questions they have asked. It is relatively simple to wallow in self-pity if you feel that the world did you wrong and you always did it right. But it's not at all easy to confront the fact that your depression is the result of childish resentment or superficial thinking.

Report Back to Yourself
All good detectives make reports and so should you. Having made inquiries about the depression and having learned some of its causes, you should then make an appointment with yourself and present the facts to yourself. Notice that there is a major difference between allowing your depressed state to talk to you and you talking to your depressed state. If this sounds a little like "gobbledygook" believe me it isn't. Even if you don't know what gobbledygook is!

Do what David did. Give your soul a good talking to! "Listen to me, soul. I've listened to your whining and moaning long enough. I've had enough of this because it is not solving anything. You have been 'cast down' long enough. You have been 'disquieted within me' far too long. It's time for something different." Before you decide that this is mind over matter, let me tell you what else David said to his soul: "Hope thou in God" (v. 5). Now that's an order!

I have met some people who couldn't drag themselves out of depression if their lives depended on it. But I have met more who could if they would tell themselves to "hope in God." When people start looking at the Lord and His attributes and abilities instead of their own failings and situations, I believe they turn the corner. But make no mistake, a definite act of the will is required!

Where There's a Will, There's a Way
I do not believe that there is *always* a way for him who has a will, but there is when it comes to dealing with depression. David thought so. Note what he said, "I will remember Him." "I will speak to Him." "I will thank Him." Everybody has a will (though

some people seem to have more of a "won't"), and this will has to be put into gear if depression is to be handled adequately. This is particularly necessary when the prevailing situation is overwhelming.

David determined to "remember" the Lord even though the very environment in which he was going to do the remembering was hostile. He only had to look around him to be reminded of the circumstances that depressed him, but he made up his mind to look away to the Lord. He had to concentrate on the Lord to succeed, but he believed God would enable him to do it.

You must learn to do this. If it is your hospital room that depresses you, make a definite decision to turn your eyes from the bed to the Bible. If it is your small children who are getting you down, turn your eyes from diapers once in a while to the crown that will be yours when they are raised to the glory of God.

Another thing. Don't keep the depression bottled up inside. Make up your mind to "say to God" what is on your heart. Say it aloud. Not because He is hard of hearing but because it is good for you to listen to what you expect Him to listen to! Start talking to Him. Make up your mind to do this. It will stop your pouting and start you moving.

The word *praise* may seem strangely out of place in a discussion of depression but it appears in a psalm on depression! So it must be fitting! "I shall yet praise Him," David said (v. 5). To understand this you must take a look at the things David said about the Lord and the special relationship they enjoyed together. His heart became so full of considerations of his God that he found his lips and his heart breaking out in praise and thanksgiving.

I know of no better cure for depression than praise. Not the empty noise that some people seem to mistake for praise. Nor do we need the evasion of truth and the escape into unreality that some call victory. But the intelligent concentration of the mind on the Lord, to such a degree that the heart becomes warm from the truth the mind is pondering, can work wonders.

Think, Don't Mope
Recently, meditation has become increasingly popular because of

the influence of Eastern religions. In our frantic western world, it is not difficult to understand why a lot of exhausted people have gone for "meditation" like salmon go for flies. There is dangerous nonsense inherent in much of this philosophy. However, this does not diminish the need for meditation.

The meditation of which Scripture speaks bears little resemblance to the mystical activities of the assorted Maharishis who have come our way. They prescribe a monosyllabic *mantra*, like "Om," on which the devotee must meditate. David had a lot more than "Om" in mind! He thought on the Lord in numerous specific ways. Moping was no longer the order of the day. His God became the focal point of his attention.

Notice carefully the details of his thought once his thinking got around to the Lord. "God of my life" came first (v. 8). It is one thing to "believe in God" but not know where or what He is. It is quite a different matter to believe that the one true and living God is "God of my life." This is a thrilling concept, for it embraces every part of a person's being. Even the part called depression.

If God is the "God of my life," presumably He is God enough to be God in the things that depress me! A broken leg may depress you if you don't believe in a God who is bigger than a broken leg. A business setback may plunge you into the depths for a month unless God is so much the God of your life that He is in reality the God of your business.

Then David talked about "God my rock" (v. 9). Now that's the sort of thing a depressed person should meditate on! When all seems lost and you have an awful sinking feeling, what could be better than to know that there is a rock beneath you upon which you can stand when you're through sinking? He can bear your weight. He will not shift position.

"God . . . is the health of my countenance" (v. 11). This is a beautiful expression. There is no doubt that a depressed person often shows on his face what is going on inside his head. But the Lord can make all the difference. He can bring health to a countenance. That means that he can so fill your thoughts that you get off yourself and your woes and get on to Him and His blessings. Then your face will change.

Some people think that Psalm 43 is a continuation of Psalm 42. The theme of depression and its antidote certainly is found in both.

"God of my strength" (43:2) is another thought that became the food of David's mind. So did "God my exceeding joy" and "God my God" (43:4). No longer filled with the poison of self-pity and morbid fixation, David is filled with thoughts of a Lord who is unsinkable and whose goodness is unmeasurable.

"Hope Thou in God

One thing remains to be said. After careful self-evaluation, self-confrontation, and self-discipline comes the direct command to the depressed soul: "Hope thou in God" (42:11). This is the final key to overcoming depression.

When a believer sinks into spiritual depression, it is because of lost hope, lost confidence, lost trust. Next time that happens to you, here's what to do:

- Examine the causes of depression.
- Remind your will of the need to act positively.
- Channel your mind into thoughts of God.
- Say to yourself: "Hope thou in God."

Get your trust where it belongs, and God will get your depression where is belongs—in the depths of the sea.

Psalm 46

God is our refuge and strength, a very present help in trouble. Therefore will not we fear though the earth be removed and though the mountains be carried into the midst of the sea, though the waters thereof roar and be troubled, though the mountains shake with the swelling thereof. Selah.

There is a river, the streams whereof shall make glad the city of God, the holy place of the tabernacles of the Most High. God is in the midst of her; she shall not be moved: God shall help her, and that right early. The heathen raged, the kingdoms were moved: He uttered His voice, the earth melted. The Lord of hosts is with us; the God of Jacob is our refuge. Selah.

Come, behold the works of the Lord, what desolations He hath made in the earth.

He maketh wars to cease unto the end of the earth; He breaketh the bow, and cutteth the spear in sunder; He burneth the chariot in the fire. Be still, and know that I am God: I will be exalted among the heathen, I will be exalted in the earth. The Lord of hosts is with us; the God of Jacob is our refuge. Selah.

11

When Your Stresses Are Greater than Your Strengths

A man went to his doctor complaining about severe headaches. He was told to stop smoking, which he did. The headaches persisted. Then he was told to stop using alcohol. He did, but the headaches continued. The doctor told him to lose weight. He did, but nothing touched the headaches. Then it was discovered that he was wearing a size 15 collar on a size 16 neck. That will give anyone a headache!

Many things can cause headaches: defective vision, poor lighting, smog, too much tobacco smoke. Some headaches come from emotional upsets. When people endure some degree of stress the body produces adrenalin, which makes more blood circulate in the brain. This in turn, causes the brain to swell inside the skull, which does not swell. Pressure builds up and headaches are the result. So stress can cause headaches literally and metaphorically. Next time you say, "My teenage son is a real headache," you may well be hitting the nail on the head!

The Impact of Stress

It should be obvious that some degree of stress is unavoidable in this world. In fact, stress is necessary if human beings are to function adequately. Many students need the stress of an examination to make them study, soldiers need the stress of a kit inspection to get themselves cleaned up, and athletes respond to the stress of the big game. But overwhelming situations can produce stress that is more than people can handle unless they are adequately equipped.

Dr. Thomas H. Holmes and his colleagues at the University of Washington have done considerable research into the whole subject of stress. They came to the conclusion that an accumulation of 200 or more "life change units" in any year may mean more disruption than an individual can stand. On their scale, death of a spouse equals 100 units, divorce equals 73 units, and Christmas equals 12 units!

When Trouble Comes

The psalmist had no scale of "life change units" to help him, but he had plenty of exposure to shattering experiences. In magnificent poetic language, he said, "Though the earth be removed, and though the mountains be carried into the midst of the sea; though the waters thereof roar and be troubled, though the mountains shake with the swelling thereof . . ." (vv. 2-3). He had his share of troubles.

He knew something of the shaking of his life as if an earthquake had hit him. His experience at times had been like a roaring swamping flood. He felt as if the very rock under his feet were moving at times. And so do many people with whom I come in contact.

I remember preaching a message from Psalm 46 entitled "When Trouble Comes." The next day a woman called and said she was in the hospital. I went to see her immediately because the news she gave me was shattering. She had been sitting in church listening to my sermon and thinking how free from trouble she and her family had been. In fact, she told me that she vaguely wondered how she would react if and when real trouble come. She didn't have to wait long in order to find out. On Monday she went for a routine medical checkup and was told she had leukemia. And she reacted according to Psalm 46!

It is obvious that all of us will have to face stressful situations at some time, so it is very important that we prepare for them. Death, illness, separation, financial problems, business worries, in-laws all play their part. Some may be more like earthquakes than others, but they all shake to some degree.

"Be Still"

It seems strange that the Lord should tell people confronted with earthquakes and floods and assorted disasters to do exactly the opposite of what their instincts tell them to do. "Run," says instinct. "Be still," says the Lord. I am not suggesting that in a literal flood you should be still or in an earthquake you should not take evasive action. But I do believe that when the troubles of life overtake us we should, instead of running away from them in hysteria, "be still."

The full statement is, "Be still and know that I am God" (v. 10).

It is not too difficult to be cool, calm, and collected when there is nothing to give you a headache. Composure is relatively simple when there is nothing to "decompose" you. But to be able to react to the unexpected in this unnatural way is difficult. So far as I know, there is only one way of doing it. That is to be so accustomed to being "still" in the Lord's presence that it becomes an intuitive reaction.

A well trained soldier will "freeze" instantly if he hears some sound that he is not expecting. It takes long hours of training to enable him to "freeze" quickly enough to save his life. That's how it is with the one who would "be still" in the Lord when the unexpected happens. I am sure that the woman I mentioned earlier was able to respond to her earthquake as calmly as she did because she had spent considerable time learning of the Lord and His ways prior to going into the hospital.

"Know That I Am God"

People do various things when they are being still. Some contemplate their navels. Others ponder mysterious questions such as "What is the sound of one hand clapping?" Some silently meditate on pyramids. Others stand on their heads. But the psalmist gives explicit instructions to people learning stillness: they are to "know that I am God."

"To know" can mean different things. Ask the man in the street if he knows the president of the United States and he will say yes. That does not mean that he knows him personally; he has probably never seen him. But it means that he is acquainted with who the president is.

To be acquainted with who God is may be a start but it is nothing more. To know Him in a personal way is what is needed. In the Old Testament the verb *to know* meant such intimacy of relationship that it was often used to describe the sexual activity between man and wife. "Adam and Eve his wife, and she conceived and bare Cain" (Gen. 4:1). It is important that we should be clear about the depth of meaning in the word *know* in the light of our rather superficial use of it.

How to Know God Intimately

Relationships don't begin on an intimate level. Intimacy develops with time and experience. So it is with the Lord. But where do you start? By realizing certain things that God has revealed about Himself. Consider the first verse of this psalm. "God is our refuge and strength, a very present help in trouble." Note the three things that God has shown the psalmist:

- He is a refuge.
- He is strength.
- He is a very present help.

To realize these things about God requires an acceptance of what the Bible teaches. This should be followed by a willingness to trust yourself to what you have accepted. To understand that God is a refuge when you are under stress is the first step. But the second step is to relate the stress to Him and seek His protecting and preserving grace. He will act on your behalf and thereby show to you another aspect of His Being. You will become aware in a practical sense of His "refuge" qualities. And accordingly, you will know Him in a fuller way.

I have been with people in situations which have become a bit awkward. These people have been able to handle the situations in such a way that I became aware of qualities in them which I had never seen before. My relationship with them in a bad situation allowed me to know them in a new way.

Unfortunately, many people do not give the Lord the opportunity to show what He can do when things get tough. As a result, they never deepen in their knowledge of Him.

"A Very Present Help"

No doubt you have experienced the nasty sensation of discovering that friends are sometimes absent in time of trouble. When all was well, they were with you. But when things started to come apart at the seams, they suddenly became conspicuous by their absence. Such people may have a tough time coping with their own difficulties and have no intention of getting involved in the troubles of others. Not so the Lord. He is a very present help in trouble.

Down through the history of the church, there have been men and women who have proved this conclusively. When the Covenanters were being hauled across the glens by the English dragoons, they took great comfort from the Psalms, not least the one that assured them that the Lord was "very present."

When Martin Luther was up to his ears in trouble with the Pope, he rejoiced in God's presence and wrote his most famous hymn, "Ein Feste Burg Ist Unser Gott" ("A Mighty Fortress Is Our God") because of the inspiration of this psalm.

Luther and the Convenanters in their moments of stress and distress came to know the Lord in a deeper dimension and so does everyone who takes the occasion to be still and know that He is God.

"There Is a River"

This psalm quite possibly was written to be sung by choirs after a great victory over enemies who threatened Jerusalem. To the people in the surrounded city the warfare had seemed like earthquakes and floods and total disaster. But now the warfare is over and the celebrating begins.

"There is a river, the streams whereof shall make glad the city of God" (v. 4). "God is in the midst of her" (v. 5).

The picture of a river in the midst of the city is very beautiful in this context. Sieges can be withstood a lot better when there is a river in the besieged city! Whatever the actual circumstances of the writing of the psalm may be, there is no doubt that the real river to which the psalmist refers is the Lord Himself. He is the river flowing to the aid of people under pressure. He it is who provides life-giving water to those who are surrounded by testings and trauma.

Delitzsch sees a parallel between these thoughts and Isaiah's beautiful words: "But there the glorious Lord will be unto us a place of broad rivers and streams; wherein shall go no galley with oars, neither shall gallant ship pass thereby" (Isa. 33:21).

What an encouragement these words are to those in the midst of shock who can take them to heart and discover the reality of the indwelling Lord in their lives and the cool peaceful flow of His water of life in their souls.

Relax and Respond

If it is true that God is a refuge (v. 1), it must be equally true that those who move into Him have nothing to fear. So they can say with assurance, "Therefore will not we fear though the earth be removed" (v. 2).

If it is true that the Lord, "is in the midst of her" (v. 5), then it must be equally true that "she shall not be moved" (v. 5).

Moving from the stage of accepting the facts of scriptural truth to the point of living in the good of scriptural truth is a "giant stride for mankind." Getting theology from head to heart so it affects the flow of blood from heart to head is the key to dealing with much of the emotional stress to which we are all subjected.

I have often told people that the pressures of the pastorate are so immense that without an adequate working theology I would doubt my ability to survive. By "working theology" I mean a belief that really believes, a faith that really expects, and a trust that really anticipates.

It is an awesome task to stand in front of a congregation week after week knowing that you are God's spokesman. When I stand in the pulpit, I know there are hundreds of people, thousands of sins, scores of needs, dozens of misunderstandings sitting there waiting in people with a host of different attitudes; and one fallible man is expected to stand before them and say, "Thus saith the

Lord . . ." I have been in many stress situations but none equals that kind of stress.

My phone rings, as it did a few minutes ago, and a man at the other end of the line says, "My mother has had a stroke and is partly paralyzed. She has pneumonia and needs antibiotics. The rest of my family say we should not give her the medication and let her die peacefully, but I don't know. What do you think I should do?"

That is stress. But do you know something? I sleep well at nights! The reason is this. I have discovered over the years that the Lord indwells me by His Spirit. He is my strength, my stronghold, and my sufficiency. Constantly I have to respond to the stress situations in which I find myself by relaxing in the Lord and responding to what I know of Him. For instance, when I have spent hours in personal and sermon preparation, I stand before the people breathing a verse of a hymn in prayer:

> "My gracious Master and my God,
> Assist me to proclaim,
> To spread through all the earth abroad,
> The honors of Thy name."

He answers that prayer and I feel the stress leave. Fully relaxed in anticipation of His blessing, I preach my heart out!

Another hymn that is continually in my thinking and praying when I am under stress is:

> "Drop Thy still dews of quietness,
> Till all our strivings cease:
> Take from our souls the strain and stress
> And let our ordered lives confess
> The beauty of Thy peace."

Review for a New View
There is a kind of reminiscence that is unhealthy. Paul knew this and said, "Forgetting those things which are behind, and reaching forth unto those things which are before, I press toward the mark" (Phil. 3:13-14).

"History is bunk," according to Henry Ford. It is a "dust heap" in the eyes of Augustine Birrell. Georg Wilhelm Hegel expressed similar, if more cultured sentiments: "What experience and history teach is this—that people and governments never have learned anything from history or acted on principles deduced from it."

JOB
JOSEPH
Still
Praised
God !

Ford, Birrell, and Hegel notwithstanding, we must insist that the history of God's dealings with people, is of immense value to those living under stress. Periodic review of what He has done is a vital necessity.

"Come behold the works of the Lord" (Ps. 46:8). The immediate application of this call has to do with the Lord's intervention in the affairs of His people and the deliverance of Jerusalem. But it is perfectly legitimate for us to take it as an invitation to review what God has done down through the centuries. Read the incidents of the Old Testament in which God showed Himself "strong in the behalf of them whose heart is perfect toward Him" (2 Chron. 16:9). Review the things that the Holy Spirit recorded concerning God's actions in the life of our Lord Jesus. In particular, the "mighty power which He wrought in Christ when He raised Him from the dead" (Eph. 1:19-20).

Then read through the Acts of the Apostles and enjoy the things that He did in establishing and building His church despite the seemingly insurmountable odds. Add to this a steady diet of missionary biographies. As you read, revel in the fact that the God of Isaac and Jacob, David and Jonathan, Paul and Silas, Luther and Wesley, Moody and Sankey is yours. That'll help the stress to go.

Selah

On 71 occasions the little word *selah* is used in the psalms. It is rather ironic that while it is so common no one is quite sure what it means. Some think it is a musical sign which gave instructions to the singers and instrumentalists. Others feel that it has liturgical significance and signaled the point in public worship where the congregation should respond.

Whatever the full meaning of the term, it is obvious that it was used to draw special attention to what had just been said. This special attention might come through a musical "forte," through a liturgical prostrating or uplifting of the hands and eyes, or even through a rip-roaring "Hallelujah!" The point surely is that the things of God as presented in psalms like this will have great bearing on our lives if we will give special attention to what has been said.

Be still therefore. Give yourself time to know God. Respond to what you know. Review what He has done and relate Him to your stresses—and see His peace reign in your heart.

Psalm 51:10-19

Create in me a clean heart, O God; and renew a right spirit within me. Cast me not away from Thy presence; and take not Thy Holy Spirit from me. Restore unto me the joy of Thy salvation; and uphold me with Thy free spirit. Then will I teach transgressors Thy ways; and sinners shall be converted unto Thee.

Deliver me from bloodguiltiness, O God, thou God of my salvation: and my tongue shall sing aloud of Thy righteousness. O Lord, open Thou my lips; and my mouth shall shew forth Thy praise.

For thou desirest not sacrifice; else would I give it: Thou delightest not in burnt offering. The sacrifices of God are a broken spirit: a broken and a contrite heart, O God, Thou wilt not despise.

Do good in Thy good pleasure unto Zion: build Thou the walls of Jerusalem. Then shalt Thou be pleased with the sacrifices of righteousness, with burnt offering and whole burnt offering: then shall they offer bullocks upon Thine altar.

12

When You Feel Like a Total Failure Because You Are

In a society where "success" is the name of the game, it's hard to be a failure. Where everybody loves a winner, losers are lonely people. But there is hope!

God Loves Failures

It ought to be obvious that the only way to become a competitive winner is to create a loser. Therefore, there have to be as many losers as winners around. Now God doesn't want to limit His affections to 50% of humanity, so he loves winners and losers alike!

But there is more to it than that! The real reason God loves losers is that there's nobody else to love! The fact of the matter is that all so-called winners are losers.

The problem is knowing a loser when we see one. We set up our standards of success, establish our own criteria, and merrily evaluate each other. But the awful thought that hits some of us is that the criteria we have chosen so arbitrarily may be faulty. Faulty criteria produce faulty evaluation, and enough faulty measurement will ensure ultimate collapse.

God refuses to be terribly impressed with dollars earned and honors gained. He has difficulty seeing the ultimate value in the number of kudos gained or orgasms achieved. But mankind is still impressed by such criteria and insists on evaluating personal success by them.

God, however, has other standards which He has consistently used ever since He produced mankind, and these criteria for evaluating personal worth need to be carefully considered. It takes little study of these standards to realize the extent to which all people have failed. But while God makes no bones about being unimpressed with human failure, He makes it abundantly clear that He has great love and concern for the ones who have failed.

You're in Good Company

Some years ago I preached a message about John Mark, the young man who went with Paul and Barnabas on a missionary journey, got cold feet, and ran away. This young man eventually became the author of the second Gospel. A striking story of God not only loving a failure but being willing to use a failure.

At the end of the service a young man who had been participating in the program came to me and said, "I have been in Christian work for years, but this is the first time I have heard that God loves and uses failures. I work in a situation where we have a constant stream of successful businessmen, athletes, movie stars, and political figures giving testimony to their faith in Christ. I got the impression there must be something seriously wrong with me because I am such a failure and they all seem like colossal successes."

It was my joy to spend long hours with that young man showing him the history book of Scripture and the way it faithfully records the failures of its heroes. Noah got drunk, Moses got angry, and Gideon got scared. Peter could be inconsistent, Paul was inconsiderate, Thomas doubted, Martha pouted. But God dealt with them and used every one of them for His glory and for our blessing.

King-size Failure

David, the king, however is one whose monumental failure is described in detail, not for our titillation but for our edification. In addition to the description of his failure, Scripture is careful to record his own account of the steps back from failure. Psalm 51, one of my favorite passages of inspired writing, gives us the details.

The psalm starts with great anguish of heart but ends with a great sense of worship and hope. The verses in between are full of truths that those who are conscious of failure should understand.

Notice that the key to David's "comeback" from the edge of disaster is the word *spirit,* which is used four times and is of great importance.

- "Renew a right spirit within me" (v. 10).
- "Take not Thy Holy Spirit from me" (v. 11).
- "Uphold me with Thy free spirit" (v. 12).
- "The sacrifices of God are a broken spirit" (v. 17).

There was a spiritual cause for David's failure so there had to be a spiritual answer. The same is true of most failure.

A Wrong Spirit

David's request for the renewal of a "right spirit" was an admission that his actions had been motivated by a wrong spirit. This is further substantiated by his acknowledgment that, before God can bless and use anyone who has failed, that person must have a "broken spirit."

A brief look at the circumstances that led to the writing of this psalm will clearly show the nature of David's "wrong spirit." Scripture records it this way, "At the time when kings go forth to battle, David sent Joab . . ." (2 Sam. 11:1). A classic case of "Lord here am I, send him!" He then went on to explain, "In an eveningtide . . . David rose from off his bed" (v. 2). Now the wrong spirit is very clearly exposed. It was a spirit of laziness! No red-blooded king stays in bed while his men are on the field of battle! The king had a case of the royal blahs.

Wise old Isaac Watts had it right when he said:

"In works of labor or of skill,
I would be busy too,
For Satan finds some mischief still
For idle hands to do."

That is exactly what happened to David. As he got up off his bed he saw Bathsheba, beautifully posed and exposed across the street. The wrong spirit took over completely at this juncture. David desired her, wanted her, sent for her, and had her. A spirit of wantonness had him by the throat.

As a result of their illicit union, the woman became pregnant.

David found himself in a real fix because Uriah, her husband, was away on active duty. David concocted a scheme for getting himself off the hook. He brought Uriah home on furlough and told him to take a few days off with his pretty little wife. But Uriah wouldn't go home. David got him drunk, and he still wouldn't go. He was a better man drunk than the king was sober!

It was then that Uriah passed the point of no return. The king manipulated his assignment and in effect had him killed in action. His sole interest was the saving of his own skin.

"Thou Art the Man"

Then God sent His prophet Nathan on a very ticklish assignment, but the prophet didn't seem too perturbed. He confronted the king by means of a story that had the king trapped before he realized the significance of it. He told David about a rich man who stole the only lamb of a poor neighbor. David boiled with rage and righteous indignation as he listened. "Thou art the man," declared the intrepid Nathan, (2 Sam. 12:7), and David broke in little pieces.

David was suddenly confronted with the immensity of his own shame and overcome with a sense of his own guilt. Some people in similar circumstances react against God's messenger. Not so David. He accepted the exposure and promptly took steps to deal with the situation.

This was highly commendable and it must be stressed that any comeback from failure necessitates honest confrontation with sin and adequate dealings with sin. There is a terrible danger that we condone the sin that God condemns. There is a possibility that we cultivate the selfishness that God repudiates. But a broken spirit is prepared to think as God thinks about these things. It is prepared to call sin sin and deal with it the only way possible—with repentance and cleansing. "Wash me thoroughly from mine iniquity, and cleanse me from my sin" (Ps. 51:2). "Purge me with hyssop and I shall be clean: wash me, and I shall be whiter than snow" (v. 7).

Coming to the point of repentance is often very hard. It is my opinion that it is made harder when we do not understand that it is the "goodness of God" that leads to repentance. David knew this for he talked of *loving-kindness* and *tender mercies,* and obviously he had a real sense of God's love and grace toward him. Not that he forgot that God deals in "truth in the inward parts" and insists on being "justified when He judges." But he was swamped by the thought of God still being prepared to love the one who does not deserve such love. This is the beauty of being a failure. God can't do much for successful people because they are so busy being complimented on their successes they have little time to see themselves realistically. As a result they feel little need for repentance. But failures have a great time being honest and realistic and loved and forgiven.

Renewal

I can vividly remember the first time I was really confronted with my own failure. It was both excruciating and exhilarating. It was excruciating because out of my love for the Lord I wanted to serve Him wholeheartedly; and yet the more I endeavored to serve Him, the more I appeared to fail Him. The more intimately I knew Him, the more intimately I got to know myself. And my self-discovery was a disappointment to put it mildly.

But it was exhilarating because I realized that I was discovering what He had known all the time. And knowing the immensity of my failure had not altered His attitude toward me one fraction. It seemed as if I had a new vision of the grace and wonder of God. He actually loved me as I was and intended to work with me as I was. Then and only then was I open to discover more of the resources that were mine in Christ. You could call my experience a "renewal of a right spirit."

This new spirit began to change many things. He would have nothing to do with laziness. He wanted to see some discipline. He hated wantonness and looked for a giving spirit. Selfishness was in total opposition to everything He stood for, so that had to die. I found myself being made new and fresh within and without.

"Thy Holy Spirit"

It is important at this juncture that we make it quite clear that the

"right spirit" of which David speaks is in essence the Holy Spirit—
or at least the product of His indwelling and outworking. This is
confirmed by the words "take not Thy Holy Spirit from me"
(v. 11).

In the days of the Old Testament the Holy Spirit used to "come
upon" people in order to equip them for specific tasks. He anointed
prophets, priests, and kings for the divine service. On occasion, if
the annointed one failed in his service and showed little or no evidence of rectifying that which was wrong, the Holy Spirit would
depart from him. This happened in the case of David's predecessor
Saul (1 Sam. 16:14). It was the thought of this humiliating experience that plagued David and stimulated his prayer. But he
need not have worried for his heart was open and warm to the
Lord and He had no intention of withdrawing him from service or
making him what Paul called a "castaway."

In our days we have a fuller experience of the Holy Spirit. Since
Pentecost, the prayer of the Lord Jesus has been fulfilled, "And
I will pray the Father, and He shall give you another Comforter,
that He may abide with you for ever" (John 14:16).

This means that a believer can settle down to maintaining a
"broken spirit" in order that he may know the freshness and beauty
of the "right spirit." The degree in which he can reject the old
spirit will have a major bearing on the way in which he can be
governed by the new spirit. Or as Paul put it, "If ye live after the
flesh, ye shall die: but if ye through the spirit do mortify the deeds
of the body, ye shall live" (Rom. 8:13).

Liberty

A boy who had been learning something of the truths contained in
this psalm said that he felt as if he had been holding his breath all
his life and now for the first time he could exhale. He was express-
ing something of the sentiments expressed in the phrase, "uphold
me with Thy free spirit" (Psalm 5:12). It was a liberating experience for him.

Free in this context does not mean "without cost." It means
"liberating." The work of the Spirit as He floods our lives is to
uphold us in a liberating experience. He has no desire to see us

permanently crippled by guilt or wretchedly broken and despairing. Guilt when dealt with, brokenness when healed, despair when banished are preludes to the liberating peace and joy that only those motivated by the Spirit of God can experience.

There is liberty from self-centeredness. This is inferred by the expression "Thy salvation." Most of the time we are so concerned about ourselves that we talk about "my salvation." It would appear that the psalmist was being very careful to acknowledge that even his salvation is the work of God. He couldn't take credit for being saved. What's more, he didn't want to take credit for anything. He was far too liberated for that kind of thing! Watch yourself for a day or two and see how often you use the word *my* when *Thy* would be much more appropriate.

The beauty of being liberated from self-centeredness is that you hold everything in much higher regard. It's one thing to talk and think about *my* house but it's much more challenging to regard it as *Thine* and use it accordingly. *My* time can be such a burden, but when it is *Thine* the days and the hours become so much more rewarding and enriching. *My* money can be such a worry, but if it becomes *Thine* it is now a matter of glad stewardship rather than constant stewing.

Freedom from Self-Trust

In a society that teaches you to be your own man and do your own thing, it is increasingly difficult not to become deluded with a sense of self-sufficiency. To some extent it is necessary for people to have confidence in their God-given abilities, but deeply ingrained self-trust leads to disaster.

No doubt David became vividly aware of the fact that he was so open to temptation and so prone to wander that self-trust was a luxury he could no longer afford. So he prayed to be "upheld." He evidently did not think it unmasculine to admit weakness. Apparently he did not feel it demeaning to his kingly role to confess inadequacy.

So many people are not free to be honest. They must "save face" at all costs. They must, if they are British, "keep a stiff upper lip." This is no problem to the liberated failure, for he has nothing to hide and is free to be open about his needs and the One who is the answer to his needs.

It is great good news that you don't have to trust your untrustworthy self but the Lord who is faithful, and it is thrilling news to know that you can be free to admit it.

Freedom from Self-interest

I am always moved when I read, "Then will I teach transgressors Thy ways; and sinners shall be converted unto Thee" (v. 13). The first thing that moves me is that this man so recently wounded and wounding had discovered such forgiveness, cleansing, and healing that he was free from his own troubles and eager to be of service to others. The second moving aspect of this verse is the fact that he spoke with great assurance: "sinners shall be converted." There is no suggestion that he had taken his traumatic experience of failure lightly; it was simply that he was aware that failure is not final.

He also became preoccupied with the affairs of Zion and Jerusalem. His thoughts turned to the possibility of the Lord being "pleased with the sacrifice of righteousness" (v. 19). To be set free from the bondage of a spiritual concern that goes no farther than the extent of your own need and to reach out to "transgressors" and "sinners" is liberty indeed. And to be free to consider the possibility of doing something that will bring delight to the Lord is exhilarating.

Freedom from Self-pity

David had plenty of grounds for guilt. There was no sin too great for him to perpetrate; yet he refused to be bound by guilt and self pity. "Set me free from these things because of the depth of Your forgiveness" is what he meant by "Deliver me from blood-guiltiness, O God" (v. 14). He had no intention of keeping his mouth shut out of shame or of hiding the truth and pretending that everything had always been well. With the freedom that only the forgiven know, he proposed to testify to the grace of God in his life. "My tongue shall sing aloud of Thy righteousness . . my mouth shall shew forth Thy praise" (vv. 14-15).

The man who lives in an aura of perpetual success and who has to maintain that kind of image is in bondage to his own myth. The self-confessed failure with the enabling, liberating spirit driving him has much more freedom and packs much more clout because of the ring of reality in what he says, does, and is.

Strange as it may seem, the way to success is failure, so don't fail to fail if you want to succeed!